Conversations with Ko Un

Conversations with Ko Un

RAMIN JAHANBEGLOO

With a Foreword by

ASHOK VAJPEYI

Orient BlackSwan

CONVERSATIONS WITH KO UN

ORIENT BLACKSWAN PRIVATE LIMITED

Registered Office
3-6-752 Himayatnagar, Hyderabad 500 029, Telangana, India
e-mail: centraloffice@orientblackswan.com

Other Offices
Bengaluru, Chennai, Guwahati,
Hyderabad, Kolkata, Mumbai,
New Delhi, Noida, Patna

First published by Orient Blackswan Private Limited 2021

ISBN 978-93-5442-022-1

038580

Typeset in
Helvetica Neue LT Std 10.5/13 *by*
Le Studio Graphique, Gurgaon 122 007

Printed in India at
Thomson Press, New Delhi 110 020

Published by
Orient Blackswan Private Limited
3-6-752 Himayatnagar, Hyderabad 500 029, Telangana, India
e-mail: info@orientblackswan.com

CONTENTS

FOREWORD

Ko Un is an amazing poet in many ways: the locale of his poetry is firmly Korean, but his explorations and insights have universality. The stubbornly local become effortlessly global. The poetic range is amazingly wide: life, human predicaments, temptations and anxieties, nature, mortality, contemplation and innovation, echoes of tradition, people, events, images of daily life, everydayness, names, symbols, metaphors, memory, etc. A poet who has suffered and served jail terms for his political views, Ko Un is yet a very gentle, civilised person whose spontaneous humanity has not been dimmed by either adversity or fame. Perhaps there is no other poet in the world who has written so much poetry as Ko Un has. He seems not only to be writing, but also embodying poetry. He once claimed that his realism was often strong in the subjectivity of the boiling point, rather than in the objectivity of the freezing point.

His knowledge of the poetry of the world is deep. For instance, talking of Paul Celan, Ko Un says, 'His preference for truth over beauty implies that he felt, in a reverse way, anxious that the beautiful expressions of language could turn into lies, the opposite of truth.' He goes on to assert that 'even now there are extreme situations being created by other forms of evil in humanity here and there'.

More audaciously, Ko Un wants to create an independent status for poetry. He aspires to develop 'an idea that poetry should be removed from among the genres of literature to be independent and be given a fresh meaning beyond literature. By doing so I want to establish a status for poetry, the oldest heritage of mankind, as a meta-art encompassing the arts in general, and so overcome this age when the novel dominates and there is a flood of non-fiction.' Ko Un goes on to underline that 'ultimately, I want to be a poem without poems and a poet without poems, and I want to write poems without a poet. I want to belong to the poem that is before or after language.'

This unusual book is a long conversation that the internationally reputed philosopher Ramin Jahanbegloo has had with the poet over a period of time and at different locations. The philosopher with deep humility and curiosity talks to the poet, and draws him to talk about his life, vision and aesthetics, travails, anxieties, and the various phases he has passed through and written in. The result is a very intense, illuminating, rich and insightful document that brings us close to a major poet of our times. It also coincidentally points out that however far away they may have gone from each other, poetry and philosophy can have a meaningful and enriching dialogue.

ASHOK VAJPEYI

ACKNOWLEDGEMENTS

I would like to take this opportunity to thank all those without whose support this work would not have been possible. At the outset, I remember with gratitude three very special people: my wife Azin Moalej, who has always kept our home smiling in my absence; Master Ko Un, who gave me the honour to have these conservations with him; and my friend Ashok Vajpeyi for having inspired with his warmth, kindness and poetic sense of life. I am especially thankful to Brother Anthony of Taizé and Professor Lee Sang-Wha for their inestimable help in translating my questions into Korean and Master Ko Un's answers into English. Last but not least, I would like to thank the incredible editorial team for their contribution to the making of this book.

RAMIN JAHANBEGLOO

INTRODUCTION
The Dance of the Poet

RAMIN JAHANBEGLOO

I first met Ko Un at the second Krakow Meeting of Poets in November 2009. My friend Adam Michnik had invited me to participate in a panel on *The Captive Mind*, a 1953 work of non-fiction by Polish poet and Nobel laureate Czesław Miłosz. Participating in the Krakow Festival was a great opportunity to get acquainted with some great poets, like Seamus Heaney, whom I had read, or to meet again Wisława Szymborska, whom I had met in 2003 during a trip organised by the Polish ministry of foreign affairs.

But meeting with Ko Un was a blessing, since I had always considered myself as a man of the East, and yet I knew so little about South Korean poetry. I was fascinated by the serene and cloudless character of Ko Un. Though he did not speak English, his friendly gestures said a thousand words.

I started reading more poems by Ko Un translated into the English and put pieces of his interesting life next to his poetry. I was hoping to meet him again and ask all the questions which were roaming in my head.

Fortunately, our paths crossed again at the Second Biennale of Asian Poetry in Delhi in February 2019. This time I brought up the idea of doing a book of conversations with him. The main reason for this was to share my own passion of Ko Un's life and work with people around the world. I wanted readers to feel the strong whispers of Ko Un's poetry within their soul. I thought that future generations could learn more about the life of this poet. I wanted to be a postman who could drop what I had learned from Ko Un in the mailboxes of people around the world.

What I have realised in reading and conversing with Ko Un over the years is that his poetry, though written in Korean, belongs to the human race. It is the heartbeat of the world, pounding on the white page of our human destiny. One can read Ko Un's poetry in translation and still feel that it was written for a European, an African, or a West Asian. All great poets speak the language of the universal. I think that is why Ko Un has been celebrated by so many poets, writers, and literary critics around the world. I'll quote just a few. Poet laureate Andrew Motion (2012) has said that Ko Un's

> hungry appetite for experience, the rapidity with which he synthesises it, the nervous energy of his rhythms: all these things are the hallmarks of a poet whose particular interest is to inhabit each moment as it passes, and yet to see all moments flowing endlessly into one another. This is the process by which he inhabits himself and other people. It is what makes him his own man, and a most eloquent citizen of the world. (Ibid.: 13)

American poet Gary Snyder (2006: *xi–xv*) says, 'Because of the purity, their nervy clarity, and their heart of compassion, his poems are not only "Korean" they belong to the world ... Ko Un is not only a major spokesperson for all of Korean culture but a voice for Planet Earth Watershed as well.'

Ko Un is a poet of immense literary achievement, with the production of 160 books so far, and more coming out shortly. He is an exceptional poet with an interesting life. Clare You (2006) epitomises it, saying,

> Ko Un is unquestionably a giant among contemporary Korean poets. His poetry is filled with memories and experiences ranging from those of his childhood to those of the senior man he now is ... he has lived as a precocious boy, a soul-searching monk, a tormented, nihilistic vagabond, a vitriolic dissident and, finally, a family man. (Ibid.: *xvii*)

Allen Ginsberg (1997: 9–11) marvelled at Ko Un, saying that he is 'finally a demon-driven Bodhisattva of Korean poetry, exuberant, demotic, abundant, obsessed with poetic creation ... Ko Un is a magnificent poet, a combination of Buddhist cognoscente, passionate political libertarian, and natural historian.'

To understand a poet's work, one must know and understand his background. Ko Un was born in 1933 in Gunsan, in the North Cholla province in Korea. He discovered poetry as an adolescent after coming across a book by the leper-poet Han Ha-Un. However, the joy of poetry did not last long; Ko Un's life was torn apart after the Korean War and there were a series of attempts to take his own life.

Ko Un turned to spirituality and became the disciple of a Buddhist monk, the venerable Hyo-Bong. It is interesting to know that Ko Un published his first poetry collection *Other World Sensitivity* in 1960 as a Buddhist monk, while he was collaborating on the founding of the *Buddhist Newspaper*. He abandoned monastic life immediately after.

'What is a poet?,' asked the great Danish philosopher Søren Kierkegaard (2000: 38). 'An unhappy man who hides deep anguish in his heart,' he replied, 'but whose lips are so formed that when the sigh and cry pass through them, it sounds like lovely music.'

Ko Un carried along with him this poetical anguish, while he continued to write poems and to teach on Jeju Island. Despite his energetic creativity and the publication of his second volume of poetry *Seaside Poems*, and other books, he decided once again to end his life in 1970 for the fourth time. He then happened to come across a worker's self-immolation, which gradually made him Korea's national dissident writer.

Ko Un established the Writers' Association of Freedom and Practice, serving as its first secretary general. He was harshly persecuted and put in prison several times, but he never stopped writing poems, travel documentaries and novels, including his famous novel *Little Pilgrim* (1991).

After being released from prison in the early 1980s and getting married, Ko Un opened a new chapter in his poetic career. A literary critic described it 'an explosion of poetry'. Ko Un began to write poems for his famous *Maninbo* (*Ten Thousand Lives*) project, in which he portrayed the Korean people he had met during his lifetime and those from Korean history. He also published a collection of poems called *Fatherland Stars* (1984), which were followed by many poetry collections and works of prose.

Ko Un was made the president of the Federation of Korean National Artists in 1989, followed by president of the Association of Writers for National Literature. After the civilian government was established, when Ko Un was allowed to go abroad, he started travelling extensively across the world, mostly on invitations from literary and poetry festivals, where he has been loved and celebrated.

In the past 30 years, Ko Un's works have been translated into about 35 languages, East and West, and his poems have been highly acclaimed and widely celebrated around the world. He has won around 30 literary prizes and honours, at home and abroad, including the Korean Literature Prize; the Lifetime Recognition Award presented by the Griffin Trust for Excellence in Poetry; the Golden Wreath Award from the Macedonia Struga Poetry Festival; and the New Golden Age Poetry Prize from the Mexico City Poetry Festival. He has been in the shortlist not a few times for the Nobel Prize in Literature.

All his life, Ko Un crossed the uneasy boundary between poet and rebel, life and death. The more he deepened the reach of poetry, the more he came closer to the essence of life. To no poet does the Delphic maxim 'know thyself' apply more profoundly than it does to Ko Un. Hence, it can be said that poetry for Ko Un is a process of becoming, whose end product must necessarily be different from its beginning. In a sense, he is the finished work of his own poetry.

Ko Un underlines in our conversations: 'Ultimately, I want to be a poem without poems and a poet without poems, and I want to write poems without a poet. I want to belong to the poem that is before or after language.'

As such, for Ko Un to write poems is to listen to the voice of the unsaid. He does not own the words; the words own him. It tells us a great deal about the relation between the being of a poet and the secret of the words. A literary critic once said of Ko Un, 'Perhaps he breathes his poems before putting them to paper. I can imagine that his poems spring forth from his enchanting breath rather than from his pen.'

Stefan George's famous verse, 'Nothing can be where the word fails', describes quite well the relation of a poet like Ko Un with his world. Such is the spiritual wealth of Ko Un's poetry: the world lies before his eyes as a land of dreams. But, of course, this is also an open rebellion against the injustices of life. All of which raise the taboo question: To what extent is writing poetry an act of dissent?

Poets have always been brave spirits, who fought against tyrannies, wars, violence, etc. In this relation, Ko Un certainly finds his place next to Vladimir Mayakovski, Federico García Lorca, Pablo Neruda, René Char and many others. Robert Hass (1999: 178) glorifies him: 'Ko Un is a remarkable poet and one of the heroes of human freedom in this half century, a religious poet who got tangled by accident in the terrible accidents of modern history. But he is somebody who has been equal to the task, a feat among human beings.'

Dissent underlines unconventionality and anti-conformism, which are the two characteristics of Ko Un's poetry. It is not violent, but it is dissenting and rebellious, like Gandhi's Satyagraha. Look at some verses of his beautiful hymn to peace:

Song of Peace

Peace is a wave,
a rolling, living wave.
Beneath that wave
swim every kind of fish.
And all kinds of coral grow.
Above that wave
no one thing is higher than any other.

It brings freedom and equality to all
as far as the sunset horizon.
The white sails speeding across that wave of peace
billow full.

Peace is rice and bread.
Before cooking, they are grains of rice or wheat or
corn.
Peace is as urgent as rice and bread.
In the ideograms of Northeast Asia, one sign for
peace
shows rice entering a mouth.
Peace begins as a day
when everyone in the world can eat.
Peace is a day when
everyone in the world eats bread together as
friends.
Banishing starvation from the earth is peace.

Poets create dangerously. Maybe that is the reason why they are always dissidents in a world of conformism and complacency. The most courageous act is to write poetry, not to make a revolution. Because, 'poetry is the music of thought', as George Steiner (2011: 12) says, and 'poetry is music of history', as Ko Un says. The poetic questioning is at its most in a poet-thinker like Ko Un.

Ko Un's influential poetry fulfils the function of a historical memory in Korea. His poetic testaments are part of today's Korean collective consciousness. At the same time, Ko Un is a universal poet; we should be careful not to turn him into an epitome of Eastern stereotype. This reminds me of what Rabindranath Tagore (1997: 90) wrote to one of his friends in Bengal, after the warm reception of *Gitanjali* in the West: 'My impression is that when a place from which nothing is expected somehow produces something, even an ordinary thing, people are amazed that is the state of mind here.'

Poetry is like water. It takes the shape of the language and culture in which it is born and later translated. So in every poem there is a hidden force, which is revitalised in a new language. It is this mutating quality of poetry that gives Ko Un's poems immortality.

In one of his poems, he writes majestically: 'When I die / I'll leave dancing'. Dance is the lightness of being, which transmutes the weight of a poet into something other than himself. And indeed, what will remain from the tears and the ashes is only poetry, and its eternal recurrence.

Delhi, June 2020

REFERENCES

Ginsberg, Allen. 1997. 'Foreword'. *What?* Berkeley: Parallax Press.

Hass, Robert. 1999. 'On Korean Poetry and Ko Un'. *Korean Culture* 20 (1). Reprinted in *What Light Can Do* (New York: Ecco, 2012).

Kierkegaard, Søren. 2000. 'Either/Or: A Fragment of Life'. In *The Essential Kierkegaard*, ed. Howard V. Hong and Edna H. Hong. Princeton: Princeton University Press.

Motion, Andrew. 2012. 'Foreword'. *First Person Sorrowful*. Northumberland, GB: Bloodaxe Books.

Snyder, Gary. 2006. 'Foreword'. *The Three Way Tavern: Selected Poems*, trans. Clare You and Richard Silberg. Berkeley: University of California Press.

Steiner, George. 2011. *The Poetry of Thought: From Hellenism to Celan*. New York: New Directions Books.

Tagore, Rabindranath. 1997. *Selected Letters of Rabindranath Tagore*. Cambridge: Cambridge University Press.

You, Clare. 2006. 'Introduction'. *Three Way Tavern: Selected Poems*, trans. Clare You and Richard Silberg. Berkeley: University of California Press.

PART I

Discovering Poetry at Gunsan

ONE

CHILDHOOD MEMORIES

RAMIN JAHANBEGLOO (henceforth RJ): You were born in Gunsan, South Korea, on 1 August 1933. Gunsan was at that time part of the North Cholla province, which was occupied by the Japanese. What are your memories of those difficult years?

KO UN: Today, we live in the Western time system, where BC and AD are connected in a linear cycle. In East Asian culture, however, we still keep a circular outlook on time, in which a one-year unit is made up of 12 different kinds of animals such as mammals, reptiles, etc., and the animals rotate every 12 years.

Every twelfth year, the year of the tiger, of the rabbit, or of the snake makes a comeback. The dragon, a mythical creature, is also among them. It was only from the twentieth century that Korean people, who had been living in a circular time system, were exposed to the linear time system made by the West.

In the early twentieth century, while Koreans still had no awareness of time scales, such as 'the twentieth century' or 'modernity', Korea fell under Japanese colonial rule far too quickly. Japan had become Westernised speedily; Korea had remained an agrarian society, where time was stagnant and people had not evolved very much from the fifteenth

Father

In his bones, Father was a dreamer,
no matter how bone-tired he was
plodding down roads to Daecheon market,
Yesan market, Seosan market,
around Nae-po across the river.
When it rained
he would hold out both palms to the rain
and rejoice, shouting: '*Aigo*! Praise be!'

—from *Maninbo*, Volume 1 (1986)

century. They perceived little difference of civilisation between the nineteenth century and fifteenth century. The Yi dynasty, which had lasted for 500 years, in such a state collapsed, turning to ashes in a single sudden blaze. I was born in a remote farm village during the colonial period.

The place I was born in was surrounded by fertile rice fields, so the name of our village includes the meaning of 'fertile', and the smaller village name means 'rice'. The name of my village, comprised of around 100 households, signifies 'a dragon resides here', representing the long-lasting agricultural society of East Asia.

Meanwhile, the farm lands that had been passed down intact to my grandfather's generation were lost when my father guaranteed a loan using the land, and so my family turned destitute tenant farmers during the colonial period.

There was an old port 4 km away from my hometown, where the ruling Japanese imperialists opened a new harbour for trade with Japan, and took all the rice produced in the region to the mainland of Japan.

Then, the Japanese were also occupying Manchuria, the north-eastern region of China, so the harbour also served as a logistics base when the Japanese army invaded the Chinese continent. Under the Japanese colonial system that took all the high-quality rice, most Korean farmers had no choice but to live in extreme poverty.

I still remember clearly how, on the nights when my family was starving, my father used to tell us, 'Tomorrow we will have rice to eat', making my family feel a little hopeful and invigorated. In spite of the extreme poverty here on earth, the night sky I gazed at was always an affluent universe.

RJ: Did you have a happy childhood or did you suffer a great deal because of the colonial occupation and Korean War?

Little Un-Tae

A child intensely shy,
shy of the world,
shy of people,
he came alive
in the gales of the last days of August.
He came alive
only when pine branches were torn away by rough winds,
when ailanthus trees were uprooted.
He came alive,
shy no longer,
his chill body blazing fiercely.
He came alive
only when his body bent in the wind like a bow,
when stones on mountain ridges went flying,
came alive with eyes sparkling and sweat beading on his nose.
For the first time he went racing along as if half mad,
as if entirely mad.
He went racing along, in tandem with the gales,
toward the end of life, toward the beginning of life.

—from *Maninbo*, Volume 2 (1986)

Note: Ko Un's original given name is Ko Un-Tae.

Ko Un: Looking back, I think I was a descendant of an old kingdom before the pre-modern times. In the village where the faces of the old men and the children were the same as they had been 500 years before, we lived with the old faces and custom. Boys let their hair grow long and plaited it on their backs. Then in the colonial period, the men were forced to cut off their topknots and the boys their plaited long hair.

Until then all the elementary education for children involved learning Chinese characters from an elderly man who had knowledge of these characters. The place was called the *seodang*, the village school. But only the privileged few were able to receive such an education, and most common kids remained illiterate.

I was fortunate enough to get an education as my father had a strong passion for learning. I was able to learn *The Analects of Confucius* at an early age. However, I was an extremely timid boy. Even when my uncle visited our house I would run away and hide myself, covering my face with my hands.

Even though it was a hard colonial period, I grew up enjoying the blessings of the dark night sky, the stars, and the moonlight that composed the ancient environment of natural communities. At an early age I experienced being moved by the natural phenomenon when the glow of the setting sun filled the wide space of the open rice fields.

There were no books in the village, but my uncle had many books on his shelves. I could read books by Goethe and found out about the Italian writer Gabriele D'Annunzio from my uncle's library. It was there that I learnt of Van Gogh as well. And after that I dreamed of becoming a painter just like him. In fact, I was quite good at drawing, so I, as a little boy, used to draw things to give as gifts, some of which were paid for by the neighbours. The drawings that I made were mostly either of tigers or of birds.

Shocked by the dropping of atomic bombs, Japan surrendered on 15 August 1945. That day was the day of our liberation from Japan. I was in the thrid year of primary school.

After graduating from the primary school, I entered a secondary school at the port, which had been a Japanese school. As the nation had just been liberated from colonial occupation, schools were wide open even to children from rural areas. Among the 500 new students assigned to eight classes, I received the highest mark in the entrance exam. In fact, that was the first as well as the last time in my life that I ranked number one.

Entering secondary school, I joined the painting club for my extracurricular activity. When I won the first prize in the school art contest, I became enthusiastic about art, and I had an ardent yearning to become an artist; I was motivated to become a painter in the future.

In the summer of 1950, when I was just 17 years old, the Korean War broke out. My hometown spent three months under the control of the North Korean Communist Party and then returned to control by the South Korean regime. During the ideological turmoil, millions of people lost their lives in the front and in the rear as well.

In my home village, leftists killed rightists, rightists killed leftists, again and again, massacring each other repeatedly. Under those circumstances I barely survived, reduced to a state of insanity.

As a naïve country boy, I experienced human brutality at an early age and found out how inhumane we humans could be. So I could find neither meaning nor value in human life. Quite often I suffered from serious mental disorders and even started to leave home.

I experienced 'futility' early on in life. The sense of futility emerged from the ruins after nature and cities were completely destroyed; my nihilism was something that I myself experienced, different from the 'nothingness' of ancient Oriental thought, or the 'nihilism' that emerged in the nineteenth century in Western countries.

Neither was it similar to the state of 'non-existence' found in ancient Eastern culture. This 'sense of futility', from that time onwards, became a part of my nature, my DNA, and served as an essential part of my life and writing.

TWO

LOVING PARENTS

RJ: What kind of people were your parents? Were they interested in culture?

Ko Un: My parents were peasants belonging to the old agrarian society, not unlike those hundreds of years before them. My mother was born in a quiet harbour town of a province located on the opposite side of the large Geum River. She had to cross the river in a boat to get married and come into my father's house in a small village. The bride got out of the boat and then rode another 5 km in a palanquin to reach her in-law's house.

I was born while my parents were working hard in the field everyday. My father, unlike most of the commoners of that time, was able to read and write through self-study. My mother was also literate with the help of my father, who taught her how to read and write the Korean letters. In the traditional Korean society of commoners, women were forbidden to learn to read and write. The simple reason was that it was a society of strict patriarchal customs, and women were not permitted to write to their parents after marriage.

My father was a dreamer. On moonlit nights, even after toilsome daily work, he used to go out into the yard and

Mother

Day long and into the evening, she'd be out in the mudflats,
ankle-deep in the vast, wretched mud of the Mangyeong River
where there were neither bones nor grains of rice.
Lugging a basketful of sea-blite, she came back home.
Why, it was already early morning,
the Great Bear had come and gone, gone!
She was utterly exhausted.
No time, though, to rest her weary body,
at once she had to hull barley in a mortar.
The pestle soared up, striking the dark sky,
then pounded down, almost piercing the ground.
Drops of sweat seasoned the barley.
Well, with that taste, the brats should grow fast.
Where else, if not here, could she sustain herself,
given so much hardship, so many bitter feelings?
A woman's life in this land surely saves a multitude of lives.

She came here to her husband's home in a palanquin
from Janghang in Chungcheong Province,
crossing muddy, slow-flowing rivers.
After that hard journey, she began her married life in a household
with not so much as a crock of bean paste or soy sauce.

dance in his bare feet. My mother was a person who rarely displayed emotions on her face. My parents didn't talk much to each other, but they had a deep trust and love for one another.

When I reached a certain age, my father sent me to the village school and used to buy me books to read. I still remember that my father was enthusiastic about reading books aloud to the neighbourhood people until very late at night. On those nights, my mother and I never failed to be among the audience absorbed in listening.

RJ: Did the fact that you were born among farmers bring you close to nature?

KO UN: In fact, the destruction of nature became serious with agriculture. The word 'culture' is derived from the word 'cultivate'. The words 'culture' and 'civilisation' take nature as an object and make it a subject matter.

However, agriculture was possible in the places surrounded by the natural environment relatively in comparison to the third industrial revolution. What's more, there was nothing but nature and so I couldn't but be close to my natural environment, although not conscious of it, while growing up under the powerful influence of nature. Even though we were poor without enough food to eat, I lived in the abundance of stars, winds, grasses, streams, and the sounds of insects, which was enough to compensate to some extent for the material poverty.

Then, during the colonial period, all the mountains turned barren as all the trees were felled by the Japanese. The lumber was requisitioned for use in the Japanese factories or as military resource. So even when the spring came, there were no azalea left to bloom on the hills. Flowerless spring was the bleak landscape of Korea during the late colonial period.

Two days after delivering her first son, she had to
pound barley,
carry food in a basket on her head to the
paddy-fields
where the second round of weeding was under
way.
She bled so much after childbirth
she had to wash her underclothes secretly five
times a day.
Her gait, though stiff as a clothes-pole, was brisk;
look, she could walk so fast and far that she stirred
an east wind.
She was so busy with every kind of job
she had no time to sing a single note
when she made it past the spring famine.
If you left the fields untended in summer,
why, that was as terrible as raising ten tiger cubs!
Living amid overgrown grass, amid poverty,
amid all those damned tasks,
my mother, my mother, how could she be only
my mother?

—from *Maninbo*, Volume 1 (1986)

I lived as a child in my home village surrounded by nature, and then in the mountains when I was a monk, and then on Jeju Island surrounded by nature, mountains, fields and the sea—my life until I reached my mid-thirties was mostly spent amidst nature.

Azaleas

Halmi-san hill used to blaze with azaleas
until I was four years old.
After that, several years running
we had to grub out the azalea roots
and burn them to heat our rooms in winter.
What hard times those were!
And no azaleas left to blossom when spring came.
When the village was poor, didn't that mean
that Halmi-san hill behind the village must also be
  poor?
Still, a few azalea roots survived.
When they were blooming,
Yang-Geum, a girl from our village,
wearing a long red ribbon in her hair,
went up to see those azaleas,
piled stones around them to make something like
  a wall,
and sat there, forgetting about home and tasks.
'Gosh! What am I doing, still here? Gracious,
  good gracious!'

—from *Maninbo*, Volume 1 (1986)

THREE

A JAPANESE EDUCATION

RJ: Did your schooling take place under the Japanese authorities?

KO UN: It did until my third year of primary school. After going to seodang, the traditional village school, I entered the modern primary school at the age of nine. That was the moment when the Japanese adopted a war footing. It was war time, when Japan invaded Manchuria and China, then charged into a war with the US and Britain when I was in my primary school.

It was mandatory for all the students to bow in the morning to the direction of the east, to Tokyo where the Japanese king resided. At noon, everyone had to mourn for fallen soldiers. When I entered the school, the Korean class, which pupils had several times a week due to the loose colonial education system until then, was abolished and all classes were compulsorily conducted solely in Japanese.

It was ironical that the child who would in future write in Korean had to grow up under an education system where it was strictly forbidden to use the Korean language. But, as I returned home, at night I could learn about our history little by little through the stories my grandfather told us in our

Headmaster Abe

Come from Japan,
headmaster Abe Sudomu
with his round glasses
was a fearsome man,
fiery-hot like the spiciest peppers.
When he stumped down the corridor
in slippers cut from a pair of old boots,
a deathly hush fell over every class.
During an ethics class in second grade
he asked us what we hoped to become.
Kids replied:
'I want to be a general in the Imperial Japanese
  Army!'
'I want to become an admiral!'
'I want to be like Yamamoto Isoroku!'
'I want to become a nursing orderly!'
'I want to become a mechanic in a plane factory
and make planes to defeat the American and
  British devils!'
Then Headmaster Abe asked me.
I leaped to my feet:
'I want to become the Emperor!'
No sooner had I spoken
than a thunderbolt struck:
'You have dared to blaspheme the venerable name
of His Imperial Majesty. You are expelled this
  instant!'
I collapsed into my seat.
But my class master pleaded,
my father put on clean clothes and came and
  pleaded,

language, and also listened to the Korean songs my mother sang from time to time.

Through strict colonial education, most of the Korean pupils were Japanised. But every night I was able to learn how to read and write Korean from a farmhand in the village. When Korea was liberated in 1945, I was the only pupil who knew how to read and write the Korean language. That enabled me to skip the third grade and go to fourth grade.

RJ: Do you have any tender memories of your classmates?

KO UN: At school, I was sometimes favoured and sometimes bullied by the students older than me. Right after the liberation, our new school principal turned out to be pro-Japanese, and so there was a campaign, a students' strike to protest against him. The boys older than me compelled me to mount on the stage and stir up the students. The incident was later reported to the government authorities, and I was not allowed to enter Gunsan Secondary School for would-be primary school teachers, even though I passed the written entrance exam, because of my misconduct.

I don't have many memories of my school friends, because I couldn't spend much time hanging out with them as I was physically weak. I am not sure whether it was due to my poor health or my out-performance in studying, but I remember that I was sometimes isolated.

However, I was very close with Kim Bong-Tae who was from a well-off family, although we competed with each other for the first rank in studying. His father was a socialist intellectual during the late colonial period. I had a glimpse of the book *Èmile* by J. J. Rousseau in his home.

During the Korean War when the leftists in the village were murdered by the rightists, Bong-Tae, along with a number of others, was taken away to a dugout made for

and I narrowly escaped expulsion.
Instead my punishment was forced labour,
sorting through stacks of rotten barley for still
  edible grains.
Every day for months amid the stench of decay
on the school's practice ground.
There, under scorching sun and beating rain,
I realised I was alone in the world.
Back in ethics class after three months of forced
  labour,
I heard Headmaster Abe repeating:
'We will win, we will win, we will win!
When the great Japanese army has won,
you peninsula people will go to Manchuria, to
  China,
and take important positions in government
  offices!'
Then a B-29 appeared, that silver four-engined
  plane.
Headmaster Abe shouted in a big voice, fearlessly,
'That's the enemy! That's a devil!'
But his shoulders drooped.
His shout died away into a solitary mutter.
Then came the Fifteenth of August.
He left for Japan in tears.

—from *Maninbo*, Volume 3 (1986)

the Japanese army during the colonial period and buried alive. After his death, even until now, I still see him once in a while in my dream.

Grandfather

No matter how far gone he was
in a drunken stupor,
two things there were he never let slip—
craftily, never let slip—
the tongue in his mouth
and the long pipe shoved in the back of his hempen
  shirt.
Every so often, when he drank a gallon of *makgeolli*,
it consumed him, and he sank
into a sodden slumber on the bank of a rice field.
Then his three sons, drunk with filial piety, came
  running
one after another and bore him home on their
  shoulders,
stumbling under his weight.
Back home, he'd have another drink,
smash down the weathered fence,
shout, 'You bitch, bitch, bitch,' in all directions,
everywhere and nowhere, 'You bitch,'
toward the red-clay field the next village over
that'd been struck by lightning a few days before . . .
then fall asleep.
Yet once he came round,
he was fresh water's thickest blood-brother:
Ko Han-Gil, standing with folded arms for the longest
  time
as though being scolded,
while rainwater fell from the rotten eaves.

Then suddenly, as if awakened by something he'd
  said:
'My boy, Japan is not our country.

Back in the old days, Admiral Yi Sun-Shin gave the
Japs hell.
So don't lose heart.'

When his family was dizzy with hunger,
he'd make a fire in the kitchen so that the chimney
smoked.
This was to deceive people into thinking
that at least his family was boiling some gruel.
Boiling nothing but water with branches of fresh pine
produced a convincingly thick cloud of choking smoke.

If offered a drink, even by an enemy of three years'
standing,
it made him happy,
made him feel rich as if he owned the sky and the
fields,
and he'd survey these fields of his
flourishing in the summer heat.
Most of the fields, true, belonged to others.
A previous year's will-o'-the-wisp came into his mind.

The name he carried in this world was empty of
meaning.
When he died, he had no tombstone inscribed with
his name.
It was enough to have 'A Commoner's Spirit'
written on the tablet at his memorial rites.
After all, what had he done with his life but study?
All he'd done was study.

—from *Maninbo*, Volume 1 (1986)

Note: Confucianism taught that male commoners lived as students during their lifetime. The spirit of a male commoner, who could never take up public office, was called 'a student'.

Dae-Gil the Farmhand

Dae-Gil, farmhand for Gwan-Jeon's family at
Saeteo,
was top-notch.
Not breaking a sweat, he could pick up a fat hog
and toss it lightly into the pigsty, squeals and all,
in the wink of an eye.
When a meal was late, he never thought to
complain.
Early each morning he would shake the dew off
and sweep and rake the village road
so it looked like a parting in your hair.

His dark eyes shone more brightly by night.
It was he who taught me to read and write Korean
under the lamplight in the farmhand's room.
So I could read the *Story of Jang-Hwa and
Hong-Ryeon*
fluently, words pouring down like rain.
A child opened his eyes to the world.
After thirty-six years of Japanese rule,
I was the only kid who could read and write our
language.

Neither his master nor other elders ever
mistreated Dae-Gil.
When we climbed up to the hill behind the village
where apricots were in blossom,
he cast no glances at the girls in thin summer
Jeogori blouses
but rested his A-frame on the ground and looked
toward the far-away sea.

I looked too, following his eyes.
We listened for the weeping roar of the rushing
  sea.

In cold winters with snow heaped high
the wind would cut through his thin shirt straight
  to his armpits.
He said:
'If a person lives in too much comfort, he thinks
  only of himself.
This world is a place where we live with others.'

Dae-Gil!
He was a light for me,
shining all night long, even as I slept.

—from *Maninbo*, Volume 1 (1986)

Bong-Tae

He and I vied for first place in grade-school.
From a rich family, he wore such nice clothes,
his five buttons always shining bright.
In his lunch box glowed a boiled egg,
and hardly any barley filled out his white rice.
Yet he was never boastful, not for an instant.
'One of our paddy-field is just beside yours.
Let's be good friends,' he said,
giving me some dried rice-cakes.
After his father committed suicide
once the Reds pulled back north,
he was dragged off by the local people,
and died in a cave in Halmi-san hill,
shot by a UN soldier.
It was a moonlit night
but he died in that dark cave.
Dear Bong-Tae,
I couldn't do a single thing to save you,
though you were sixteen as I was.

—from *Maninbo*, Volume 2 (1986)

FOUR

THE LOVE OF POETRY

RJ: Did you start reading and writing poetry at a young age?

Ko Un: No. I didn't even know what a poem was. After I entered secondary school right after the liberation, I first encountered poetry when I read poems in the school textbook.

It was a poem named 'Vast Plains' written by Lee Yuk-sa. He was an underground fighter for Korean independence in China during the Japanese colonial period, and died in a Japanese military prison in China during his sixteenth imprisonment.

There was such a colossal world in that poem, composed of the great spaces he called the 'vast plains', the vast time of the ancient days when the world began, and his 'great man riding on horseback' might be the same as Nietzsche's 'Superman', a notion which absolutely overwhelmed me as a boy. Poetry scared me. Not knowing what poetry was I just encountered a poem, which is like being born without knowing who my father is and who my mother is.

After the Korean War broke out I started writing poems. I used to write poems hanging around with Kim Ki-ho in my village who was six years older than me. When my father

Han Ha-Un

When the 1940s were nearly over
and I was in the second year of middle school,
I was making the two-mile journey back home,
trudging along at dusk.
Approaching the Mije crossroads,
I suddenly noticed something
lying in the middle of the road.
My heart began to beat hard.
I picked it up.
It was a book,
a poetry book,
by Han Ha-Un, a leper-poet.

'On and on, a yellow-clay road ...'
Home,
I read it again and again, through the night.
I also read the commentary at the end by Jo
Yeong-Am,
several times,
and the commentary by Choi Yeong-Hae, too.

From that day on, I was Han Ha-Un.
From that day on, I was a wandering leper.
From that day on, the world was to me a yellow-
clay road.
From that day on, I was a poet,
a sorrowful poet with no eyebrows.

—from *Maninbo*, Volume 7 (1989)

and I fled to Gogunsangundo Island near my hometown during the war, I used to scribble poems all day.

But after that, I became a monk, and poetry was out of my life for a while.

RJ: When did you decide to be a poet?

Ko Un: Since I happened to learn about Van Gogh at an early age, I dreamed of becoming a painter. As I told you before, in secondary school, as a member of a painting club, I worked hard on drawing after school, from 3 pm until 5 to 6 pm. My art teacher was also ambitious about making me a painter in the future.

One late afternoon in the spring of 1949, after finishing practice in the art club, I was walking home along the road that was about 4 km long. On the roadside, I found a poetry book, so I picked it up.

It was a brand new book that someone seemed to have purchased and lost on the road. It looked as if it was waiting for me. I returned home carrying it and found that it was written by a homeless leper. The poems were heartbreaking, describing how his rotten toes dropped off one day and all his eyebrows fell out the next. The poems were about his sad journey along the road to the lepers' village far away.

I wept all through the night reading the poems. I was so touched that I wished I were the leper myself. I then decided to become a wandering poet writing heartbreaking poems like him.

However, I kept it to myself for quite a long time.

FIVE

THE KOREAN WAR

RJ: As a teenager, you were emotionally sensitive to what was happening around you. Did the atrocities of the Korean War and the mortal conflict between the nationalists and communists which came later affect you as a poet?

Ko Un: My generation had to undergo an extremely turbulent history; it might be considered accident or fate. My boyhood began in the dark period of Japanese colonial rule, then came the invasions and wars, of Japanese militarism expanding to every region of Asia leading to the five years of the Second World War.

Then, I had to go through adolescence in the years of the division of the Korean peninsula, leading to the extreme situations of the Korean War. More than 3 million people lost their lives during the Korean War, including half of my generation, both in the North and in the South, and somehow I managed to survive.

During the Korean War, people in the rear were no different from those at the front, divided into two, right and left, and constantly killing one another. I barely managed to survive the age of blood and graves. Having survived meant that I was left with some trauma, wounded in body and mind. After that time, I always felt the weight of those

Others' Eyes

That war
took away the greetings we used to exchange even
with strangers.
It took away customs of speaking slowly,
gently.
Words became faster
and sharp.
That war took away the clarity in the eyes
of people in autumn's cool wind.
Gradually,
not only the eyes of people
but of cows and horses in the stony fields
grew bloodshot and fierce.

In front of Daejeon Station
a gum-selling kid
was clearly beating another kid to death.
Not one spectator
intervened. The wind stirred up the dust.

Not one
had the friendly face of villagers back home.

—from *Maninbo*, Volume 16 (2004)

who died prior to me on my shoulders, and I had to live submerged in pessimism about life without any desire to go on living.

For quite a long time, my consciousness was filled with terms such as death, futility and despair. My unconsciousness was not so much different from my conscious state. Such inner factors must be, after all, at the bottom of the ecosystem of my poems.

RJ: Did you lose many relatives and friends in the turmoil of the Korean War of 1950–53?

Ko Un: I still suffer from guilt that I was unable to prevent people from killing my innocent friend who, as I told you, I was close to in my home village. I lost almost all of my relatives.

It was inevitable that I had a deep sense of loss of myself who survived the ruins of the 1950s. I was only 20 years old then, and I had to live as an orphan of the age in the reality of ashes and ruins as if I had been an orphan in the infinite universe.

Even today, when I visit some of the big cities newly constructed, I often hallucinate that the high buildings are collapsing and turning into ashes. My mind is filled more with nothingness than with being. So I consider that the post-war era was a time of destitution that started again from nothingness.

RJ: Was it because of these losses that you decided to commit suicide?

Ko Un: I witnessed so many deaths that those who had died permeated into my life without my being aware of it, and whenever I was obsessed with the sense of the futility of life, I attempted to commit suicide with thorough preparations. The suicide attempts that first began in my early twenties

Commie 2

I was no commie.
One day I met my kid's school teacher
and bought him a drink
in the tavern at the junction.
As we were drinking a measure of *makkolli*, then
another half-measure,
the school teacher
praised my kid saying
his grades were so-so
but he was good at stopping kids fighting.

Then, pinching the wrinkles between his
eyebrows,
Mr Kim said:

In future,
the time will come when everyone lives equally
well.
The land will not belong to landowners
but to all who farm it.

I lost all taste for liquor and opened my eyes wide.
Inside the tavern
there was an old woman
and two other drinkers.

A few days later I heard
that a plainclothesman was coming to arrest me.
The village head shook his head:
Strange,
strange.
You're no commie.

continued, in all, four times until I reached my late thirties. However, an unexpected incident at each attempt saved my life, which I still consider unusual coincidence.

RJ: Today, when you look back, how do you evaluate this suicide attempt? You lost hearing in one ear because of it.

KO UN: In my late twenties I was so frustrated with the sounds and languages of the world that one day I poured potassium cyanide into my ears. One eardrum and acoustic nerve melted down and it became permanently deaf. The other ear was saved as I lowered my head to one side by instinct because of the burning pain and it instead burnt one cheek. This was a self-harming action, different from a suicide attempt.

Nowadays, the global increase in suicide rates is considered to be an important social issue in Korea as well. Yet, back then, it was considered a very philosophical or literary act.

I was scared.
I escaped to my wife's home several miles away,
then moved to another house.
I kept moving around,
as I hated being a burden to other people.

Then a man told me he was on his way up into the
 mountains,
so I followed him.
I was no commie.
Then, eventually,
I became a commie.

From Jiri Mountain I used to look toward home,
longing to go back down.
Longing to go back down.

—from *Maninbo*, Volume 16 (2004)

Ruins

When I was just twenty,
everywhere I went was in ruins.

During the nights of curfew,
wide awake, I often inclined more to death than to
  life.

Ruins didn't easily change
into something.
They didn't change into something,
and weren't born to cry as other babies.

The war did not end in my heart.

Fifty years later
I saw the ruins in this city.
I was still a piece of broken brick in the ruins
in this ostentatious city.

The oil-lamp lights of those days are gone now,
but the post-ruin age has not reached me.

—from *Belated Songs* (2002)

SIX

IN SEARCH OF SPIRITUALITY

RJ: Was it after you returned to life again that you decided to turn to *Seon* (Zen) Buddhism?

Ko Un: It was not to pursue some truth and to reach a profound state with a special religious intention that I turned to Buddhism right after the Korean War in the early 1950s. After the Korean War, I worked as a checker in the logistics department of the US Corps, headquartered in Gunsan harbour.

And then I was specially employed to teach Korean at a private secondary school owned by my distant relative. But I still suffered from mental disorder and breakdown. In my late teens, when I walked along the street, people would point at me saying, 'He's insane.' My behaviour must have been very strange and I often left home and went wandering around until my father caught me to bring me home.

Then, one day, I bumped into a travelling Buddhist monk on the road, who was very intelligent and captivating. I just followed him without thinking, like a piece of iron drawn to a magnet. The monk tried to drive me away several times but he eventually accepted me as his companion.

I learned from him the illogical leaps of Seon and absorbed his wide and profound thought across all ages

Haze

Haze.
Haze.
The meditation room of Mirae-sa temple was in a
cave
located halfway up Mireuk Island off Tongyeong,
South Gyeongsang Province.

Haze.
Haze.
Haze,
whimpering
around the islands of the southern sea.

A flight of day-flies
was growing drunk in the milky air.

Multi-coloured blossoms, too, intoxicated.

Inside the meditation room
Master Hyo-Bong and his main disciple, the monk
Il-Cho
performed morning meditation sitting
cross-legged.
After a break for powdered pine needles mixed in
cold water,
afternoon meditation.

Haze.
Haze.

Abruptly
the twenty-three-year-old Il-Cho stood,
picked up a piece of heating flue
and smashed it down:

and countries as water permeates parched ground. We wandered around together, sometimes practising Seon on the road. Then one day he decided to return to the world and sent me to a remote temple by the South Sea.

There I met the great Buddhist monk Hyo-Bong and became his disciple. Wild, furious waves finally met deep and unyielding waves.

RJ: Did spirituality open new dimensions to your life and to your poetry?

Ko Un: Christian spirituality is not exactly correspondent to the spirituality of Eastern philosophy. Nonetheless, the two share some common features in that they both grasp the stage of the enlightened mind through practice: I mean when we do not take into account the difference between autonomy and heteronomy.

I am aware, though not always conscious, that the acute angles of my natural sensitivity and the experiences of Seon practices are reflected in my poems, and I also know that they are at the base of my artistic impulse.

While living as a Buddhist monk I, at first, concentrated on learning the scriptures. Then I shifted to practising Seon, dedicating a certain period of time to intensely concentrating on it. I devoted myself to pursuing the truth, one time fasting for three weeks and at another without sleeping. I am not sure whether such religious practices effected any drastic transformation of my mental state, though there were several instances when I enjoyed the brimming self-satisfaction.

The immersive experiences in that period must have embedded in my flesh and bones. Part of them must have become my blood and then must now be embodied. However, Seon, in fact, makes us watch against our being content with such experiences.

'Master, what good does it do to become a Buddha?
I'm giving up this goddamn meditation.'

Master Hyo-Bong quietly opened his eyes.
Far from scolding with a thundering voice,
far from beating him hard with his stick,
far from drubbing him with the words of Master Imje
or the words of Master Deoksan,
he beamed:
'Why, yes, what good does it do to become a
goddamn Buddha?
Let's drop it.
Let's drop it now.'
He unfolded his legs and
sprawled out flat on the floor.

'What?'

Il-Cho fell prostrate, bursting into tears.

'Master, forgive me, please.'

Master Hyo-Bong cheered his disciple:

'OK then,
let's get back to studying.'

Haze
aze
ze
e

—from *Maninbo*, Volume 28 (2010)

Note: Il-Cho was Ko Un's Buddhist name, received from Master Hyo-Bong, that he used while he was a Buddhist monk, 1952–62. Hyo-Bong was a judge in the Japanese period who resigned and became a famous senior monk. He took Ko Un as his main disciple and companion.

I believe that I ate and digested all those Buddhist experiences I had at that time. I sometimes say metaphorically that if I had not digested what I had taken in during those days, I would suffer from indigestion by now.

Now I take the complete nothingness and emptiness that denies any substance as the true nature of my life. Simply put, nothingness is the root of my mind. Poetry too is, to me, nothing other than the rhythm of nothingness.

Teacher and Pupil

An elderly monk was sitting on a rock.
A youthful monk approached him.

'How should I live?'
'Live in the way a deer beholds a spring of water.'
'That's very good. But I,
I want to live in a slightly different way.'
'How do you want to live?'
'Suppose I lived in the way a spring of water
  beholds a deer?'
'That's very good. I want to live like that too.'

The elderly monk jumped up from the rock.
'From now on you are my teacher.
I am your pupil.'
The young monk rejoiced, showing all his teeth.
'Aha, my first disciple!'

A tiger was watching them from on the hill.

Does it have its eye directly on them,
or is it just looking?
Quickly, now, speak up;
do you want to live in the way the tiger beholds
  you?
Or do you want to live in the way you behold the
  tiger,
startled out of your wits?

—from *Maninbo*, Volume 24 (2007)

SEVEN

SUICIDE AND AFTER

RJ: However, you left the monastic life in 1962, and in 1970 you attempted suicide a second time. What went wrong? Did you feel that your life was meaningless?

Ko Un: Since my boyhood when I went through the Korean War, death was clinging to me until 1970. The suicide attempt in 1962 on the sea off Jeju Island was due to my sense of meaninglessness and renunciation because I failed to adapt myself to the reality after having returned to the secular world. The despair that I felt that I was not capable of harmonising with society must have made me abandon myself, oppressing myself to the thought that I was all alone in the world. In 1970, I made the fourth and the final suicidal attempt, and it failed.

RJ: And yet, you had published your first book of poetry, *Pian-gamseong* (*Other World Sensitivity*), in 1960. So, in a way, poetry was with you, despite depressions and difficulties?

Ko Un: I was still a monk when my first collection of poems *Other World Sensitivity* was published in 1960. At that time I was dimly aware that poetry would be my way. I thought that writing and religion would be in harmony with each

A Poet's Heart

A poet is born in a corner of this world,
between the chinks of crimes
such as larceny, murder, fraud, and violence.

A poet's words arise between the chinks
of abusive, vulgar oaths in the lowest slums,
and live for a while in society.

The poet's heart shapes a brief outcry of truth
  from his age
that comes leaking out from the chinks of evil and
  falsehood.
Then that heart
gets beaten to death by other hearts.

A poet's heart is ultimately unfortunate.

—from *Other World Sensitivity* (1960)

other. However, that kind of relief was only on the surface, and I later learned that there was still a gloomy metaphysics hidden in the depth within me.

I realised that I depended for my life on the world of poetry and that poetry too was not a comet that would fly away from me, but the relation between me and poetry would continue permanently with a gravitational relationship in which one becomes a planet and then another a satellite. That conviction still resides as a cause deep in me.

T. S. Eliot once said something like 'a poet begins in his thirties'. I, too, was able to achieve a certain level of poetic maturity after many years since I made an official debut as a poet at the age of 25.

RJ: Have you ever lost the taste of writing or reading poetry?

KO UN: I meet poetry more often in the state of unconsciousness than of consciousness. When poetry comes to me, I write it down, and when it doesn't, I don't. I would say that my heart is only an instrument to my hands. My hands are my soul.

Only, I live in a poetic state at all times. It is as if pieces of light are spread on my life like the ripples reflected twinkling on the wide stretch of water at sunset.

I am quite inexperienced with karmas other than poetry. That is the reason why I am often in need of my wife's protection.

Poetry Left Behind

If it's possible, if it's really possible,
why should there not be times when we wish to
start again
from mother's womb
as a new-born baby.
Life always has to listen alone
to the sound of the next wave.

Still, we should not turn back from the road once
taken.
Fragments of the years while I wandered about
are flapping like laundry
here and there.

When I was poor even tears were lacking.

Some nights
I warmed my cold back at a dwindling bonfire
then turning in the blank darkness, warmed my
breast.
Some other nights
I simply froze, and shuddered trembling.

Whenever countless tomorrows became today
I was often a stranger in a back seat.
At dusk the hills were standing in serried ranks
and the road I must take
seemed longer than that which I had taken.

The wind was blowing.
The wind was blowing.

Sorrow is never something we sell or buy.
So, be sorrowful

as a lamp
far away.

There should be nothing that I have left,
but feeling there was something
I have left behind
I rose quickly from the spot where I had been
   staying.
That was probably near the outermost tip of
   Tae-an Peninsula
on the west coast as fog was lifting.

Was that a spirit howling once, or poetry?

—from *Poetry Left Behind* (2002)

EIGHT

MEETING WITH POETS

RJ: What poets were you reading in those days?

Ko Un: I read poems by Li Po of ancient China and Dante of Italy in the medieval times from time to time. I also read some modern Persian poems. But as I was more dedicated to the life of a Buddhist monk, I didn't have many chances to read poems written by others.

In the early 1960s, I put an end to my life as a monk and returned to the secular world, and then left for Jeju Island. The only thing I brought with me was a collection of poems by Mallarmé. At the time I left for Jeju Island, Mallarmé and Valéry were the poets I was fond of. I stayed on Jeju Island for three years and published two collections of poems. Then I left Jeju Island.

RJ: Did you feel close to non-Korean literature? Who were the poets that impressed you?

Ko Un: When I became a poet, I was almost ignorant of Korean poems, not to mention poems of the world. I didn't become a poet after reading some poets' poems. I would say, I first started as a blind or a deaf person, and then, starting with my own poems, poetic images of the world began coming in and out of my senses and consciousness.

Sleep

No matter how deeply I sleep
the moonlit night
remains as bright as ever.

If I wake with a start
turn
and nestle down again
once my eyes have closed
the moonlight trapped inside them
becomes part of me.

But are the clouds washed pure?
Pure enough for the moon as it drops behind the
western hills?

Now my sleep is a shadow of sleep,
as a shadow cast on a moonlit night.

—from *Other World Sensitivity* (1960)

I only knew some of the regional poets, not even knowing Kim So-Wol, the genius of modern Korean poetry.

It was in the 1960s that I was finally introduced to and fascinated by Baudelaire, Mallarmé and Valéry by Korean scholars of French literature. I also got to know Byron, Goethe, Hölderlin and Rilke.

In the 1970s, I met Mayakovski, Neruda and Lorca. In the 1990s, I was attracted by Borges. I was oddly shocked when Borges severely criticised Tagore and called him 'a swindler'.

My late friendships with Allen Ginsberg, Gary Snyder and Robert Hass of the US, Michel Deguy of France, Tomas Tranströmer of Sweden, Antonio Colinas of Spain, and Breyten Breytenbach of South Africa are special. Among them, Snyder and I refer to each other as 'brother-poets living on the opposite side of the earth', and miss one another.

NINE

POETRY AND POLITICS

RJ: You seemed to be touched and influenced by the everydayness of Korean politics and yet poetry escapes from everydayness. Yves Bonnefoy, the French poet, used to say, 'Poetry is a continuous search which could help us in the construction of a society based on truth.' Do you believe in this?

Ko Un: Yves Bonnefoy's discourse is intense. He, however, doesn't seem to leave any traces behind in thinking and improving the matter of reality as an activist. When I met him at College de France, he said that the world of my Buddhism and the world of Mallarmé could be connected at an approximation. He was indifferent to my engagement in relation to the democratic movements or the Korean Unification movement in Korea. Bonnefoy leads me to comment that in France I confront language rather than life. France doesn't seem to exist without words. In France even silence becomes a cultural heritage of languages.

I do not have the courage to connect poetry to the task of making society grow with a sustainable capability in politics and economics. But I do believe that poetry can exert its dramatic power to transform our society and

Road

When I see a road
I feel that there is a place I need to hurry toward.
When I look at a hamlet like Sinyoung-ri or Nae-ri,
I feel that there is somewhere I have to go beyond
that hamlet.
Truly! Neither a by-way in Majeong-ri
nor the sixty-mile road to Janghowon
allows me to go to sleep easily.
When I see a road
it inevitably makes my spirit soar.
I must go.
I must go.
Don't ask where I am going.
At its end the road turns into a country.
I have to go to that country.
I exist
in the nation of people who climb up and down
the rough Chuga-ryeong Pass all their lives.
I have to take
every road in both South and North.
There is a road that finally leads to one single
country.
I must go.
I must go.

—from *Fatherland Stars* (1984)

create a social soul. I think the popular poets of Russia are another Trotsky.

Lorca who was sacrificed at too young an age arouses the practical sympathy of the world with his poems after his death. Neruda was the same. The issue of whether poetry corresponds to truth can be found more in Hölderlin's autism than in Goethe's whole man. It would be much better to find it later in Bertolt Brecht who fought against the falsehood of all sorts of regimes.

RJ: And yet, in the 1970s you became actively involved in social and political causes, and because of your activism you went to prison several times. You remind me of Lorca, Aragon and Neruda, all different poets from different cultural backgrounds who felt the necessity of getting engaged in politics.

Ko Un: In Latin America, I am referred to as the 'Neruda of Korea'. In China, the 'Li Po of Korea', in Germany, the 'Goethe of Korea'. In France, I am humbled to be referred to as the 'Victor Hugo of Korea'. A poet of India called me the 'Tolstoy of Korea'. However, such temporary nicknames are the expressions of kindness and admirations to a visitor out of hospitality, emphasising one side of my literary creation and life. I am ultimately the Ko Un of nothingness and the nothingness of Ko Un.

I do not consider it a poet's necessary destiny to engage in reality, or sacrifice himself or herself. A poet is a being who can have many different destinies. There can be cases in which a poet's life has faces of multiple poets. In my case I am no more a poet as in my twenties, and I cannot be pinned down as a poet in my forties, and in my eighties I am and shall be in another world of poetry. One divides in perpetuum, and multitude is nostalgic of being one. Just like the universe.

193

These are my beliefs:

I believe in morning dew.
I believe in the rain that will come a few days later.

I believe in the wind.
I believe in the smell of shit
borne on the wind.
I believe in gangsters' nights.

I believe not in truth
but in the fact that the truth changes.

Now, with my scepticism
I believe that there is nothing at all to believe in.

My belief is something else again.

—from *Untitled Poems* (2013)

Passing through the 1970s and 1980s of the last century, I was never indifferent to the task of the social engagement of poetry. I stayed away from personal values and non-political inclinations, away from the problems of reality.

Then, from the 1990s, I encountered a new self which was pursuing a world of other dimensions. Naturally there was an awareness at the bottom of my move that our social and political situations were no longer very desperate.

I realised that family is as important as the dignity of society. Also I came to feel acutely the beauty of clouds and the night sky as much as I did the value of land. Poetry is to me sky, land, and day and night. I call it a 'psycho-physical rotation'.

I see myself more overwhelmed by non-political universal phenomena than by politics. I still read Carl Sagan from time to time. Even so, my perception and diagnosis of reality as well as my political sense have never become dull.

PART II

Elective Affinities

ONE

RUINS AND ASHES

RJ: Your first collection of youthful poems, *Other World Sensitivity*, was published in 1960, while you were still a monk. When you look back at these poems, do you still feel a proximity with your spiritual experience, or is it a closed book?

KO UN: My first collection of poems, *Other World Sensitivity*, was in fact my second poetry book. The initial title of my first poetry collection, comprising about 30 poems, was *Triangle Poems*, and the title was later changed to *Fire Moth.* It was sent for printing, but the printing shop caught fire just before printing began and all the manuscripts were burnt. As I hadn't made copies of those poems I lost most of them.

My first memory of the fire goes back to when I was around six years old. Our house was completely burnt down, turning the main building, with its four small living spaces, into ashes. I still vividly remember the scene as my mother dug spoons and brass pots out of the ruins.

The memory of that first fire overlapped with the burning of my first poetry collection to ashes. It also seems to be a metaphor of how I survived as a youth from ruins and ashes.

Ode to Cheoneun-sa Temple

They live
among themselves.

Below the valley and above it
their spirits float,
heard as wind.

Now they are
a sound of wind in pine trees at night.

Look rather at the rocks
on the empty hillside.

Autumn has come
to the weeping tinkling of a wind-bell
at the end of an angle rafter that
chose to sit on a rock.

Having gone back to the world and quite forgotten
  about them,
now I long to go back
to the hillside where the wind of their spirits drifts.

They
live.

They
live.

—from *Other World Sensitivity* (1960)

Note: When Ko Un wrote this poem in the 1950s, Cheoneun-sa Temple was a Buddhist temple for nuns only.

The poems in *Other World Sensitivity* were written in spare moments while I was concentrating on Seon practice, such as fasting in Haein-sa Temple, one of the major Buddhist temples of Korea. It was well received and acclaimed by a number of poets in Seoul. Some extravagantly praised me as the 'Tagore of Korea'.

However, I was not satisfied with the poems in that collection. It seemed to me that some of them were a little bit too religious while others a little bit too worldly.

Many years later a French poet, Alain Jouffroy, wrote about me, in a poem he dedicated to me, that 'Ko Un is a Ko Un Mandala'. I think that the world of my poems was already not restricted to a specific field but encompassed a necessary blend of various colours and many dimensions. Perhaps this has fostered into how my poems now accompany the astrophysical sentiments and the consciousness of particle physics.

In the early 1960s, after I returned to the secular world, I lived at two contradictory extremes, self-torture during the day and self-intoxication at night. And I was aware that such self-contradictions and 'selfhood' were absolutely nothing but fictions, the result of the desire that continues the transience of life and the agony of life.

I was not in the line of the Buddhist *Diamond Sutra*; rather I kept ruminating on the meaning of life through existential contemplation. Perhaps from that time I might have instinctively resisted the modern concept of self-consciousness.

There's no poet in this world who is not captivated by spiritual things, by the soul. I, too, was uncontrollably fascinated by such things and my religious sentiments were sometimes well elevated.

However, after realising that meaning was mere expression of meaninglessness, I started to be more

254

Lu Xun's 'Absentee,'
Borges' 'Invisible Man,'
the 'Nastika' in the ancient Indian Code of Manu,
all signify 'one who does not exist.'

The reason the Brahman is wonderful
is indeed
that it too is another name for the void.

I have been to
so many places in the world.
I have been in many different ages
of this world.
I am modernity,
antiquity, and prehistory.
I have been the world's north, south, east, and west.

Indeed, I should return to the body
wandering between life and death,
with nowhere to come and go,
right away from tomorrow.

—from *Untitled Poems* (2013)

interested in the unconsciousness or the movement of the micro-physical world as the reason of this world than in spiritual things.

Eventually my thought reached the conclusion that there is no distinction between mind and material, no distinction between particles and energy. Furthermore, I sometimes think that maybe it's my body that makes up my mind.

Still, the world of poetry is more a world of mystery.

RJ: You published your second and third volumes of poetry, *Seaside Poems* and *God, the Last Village of Language*, respectively, in 1966 and 1967. However, this was a very dark period of your life marked by a drinking habit. Did you ever think of abandoning poetry and stop writing poems?

KO UN: Two collections of poems were published in succession after the first poetry collection published in 1960. In 1964, I decided to commit suicide at sea and took a boat from Mokpo, crossing the Jeju Straits. But being intoxicated with the moonlight, I drank so much that I fell asleep on the boat, forgetting about committing suicide. At that time I didn't know that people don't get drunk while at sea. By the time I woke up, I found that I had arrived on Jeju Island in the Southern Sea.

A friend of mine in Seoul published the poems I wrote while I was living on Jeju Island for three years. Considering the condition of publication in Korea at that time, it was extremely rare to have poetry books published.

Even now I am sometimes fond of the flow of abundant linguistic sentiment, like the overflowing tide of the sea in my second collection, *Seaside Poems*.

God, the Last Village of Language was published in 1967 when I returned to Seoul after my three-year stay on Jeju Island.

A Poem

One day
it was a guest.

One day
it was the host.

All those years
each of the chimneys was dreaming
of the smoke it would send up.

Today I'm still not sure who a poem is.

—from *Belated Songs* (2002)

These two poetry collections were the products of the period when, after my return to the secular world, I suffered from a chronic existential state of despair as well as extreme insomnia. On these countless sleepless nights, I was haunted by hallucinations, such as, that I was a man on night duty for the world or that I was an orphan or a man lost in the universe. Despair gave birth to an abnormal temperature of language.

In those days I was tempted to give up writing almost as a seasonal illness. In the 1960s, it was due to my anti-social way of living, and in the 1970s, it was because of my intense resistance against the harsh military regime in Korea.

Poetry, by its nature, may be born with the halt of the last poem. So I believe that poetry is destined to inherit the genes of matriarchal society. The source of poetry resembles the womb of a mother who gives birth to yet another child while her newborn either dies soon or keeps growing.

Ode to Cemetery

Although no one comes to visit you now,
your descendants will be coming, one by one.
Last night, the last insect crying on after the rest
made the night darken!
This autumn morning, you're asleep, drying
precious dewdrops.
As sunlight comes down further off, it makes the
grass tips look white.
Near the place where pasque flowers bloomed in
early spring,
wild chrysanthemums I've awaited for days bloom
in clusters.

All you once treasured has vanished in about the
same way,
while several tombstones live standing, as if
surprised.
Even though your bones cry out like rooks'
feathers,
in this world where you once lived, this autumn
may not be so very sad.
It is only a man still alive, nay, only a man who has
lost something
whom the autumn makes wander along the
mountain trails without houses.
Neither temples nor bell sound from temples
should be there.

When you completed your lives in this world,
you only left behind your small anniversaries.
There are no past days in this world,

you are simply awakening presentiments of past
days.
By chance, perhaps by mistake, a yellow butterfly
flies low over a grave,
keeps saying that there are also graves up there in
the sky.
Although no one comes visiting you now, you
simply lie here in your graves.
Your descendants will be coming soon.

—from *Seaside Poems* (1966)

TWO

MEETING WITH DESTINY

RJ: What changed your life? Was it the self-immolation of Jeon Tae-Il, a young garment worker?

Ko Un: The glow of the setting sun one afternoon may transform one's life, and one day's windstorm or breeze may change one's way. Change sometimes requires dramatic momentum, but at other times, it can sneak in one, unnoticed, like a thief, in our daily life amidst the seasons, transforming 'I' into another 'I'.

I cannot define simply that it was a certain inevitability that changed me, from being the eight-year-old 'I' to being the 'I' of 16 years old. There must have been countless nets of relationships that touched or reached me like the sound of the wind brushing against the rim of my ear, and I have no reason to try to find out to which string among them all my eardrum's soul responded and moved me to change.

It was a coincidence that I came upon the news of the incident of a worker's self-immolation in the winter of 1970. At that time Korea had curfew, and one day I was drinking alone in a *baraque* bar (a temporarily built bar in decay) located in downtown Seoul after it was closed; I fell asleep on the table. I was allowed to do that probably because the owner of the bar was either generous or pitied me.

Jeon Tae-Il

His death
was your beginning,
my beginning.
We gathered by ones and twos,
it was the beginning of the morning sea,
in haze.

He was our beginning even in the dead of night.

—from *Maninbo*, Volume 10 (1996)

Drunk, I tumbled down to the floor and felt very uncomfortable. Then I woke up early in the morning owing to thirst. I happened to read a short report of one paragraph about a worker's suicide a few days before, among the newspapers scattered on the floor.

It was about a worker who had set fire to himself, calling for improved working conditions. It was exceptional that such a report was found in the newspaper, even as a small article, because all the newspapers were under government censorship. In spite of the discomfort of the hangover, I was struck by the news and suddenly sobered up.

I started to compare that worker's death to my own almost habitual suicidal urge. That led me to turn my eyes to the appalling reality of labour as well as to the structural contradictions of Korean society. Through extensive reading and thinking until late at night, my interest expanded to our people, our history, and our present society.

I came to realise that my sense of nothingness and futility had continued for far too long. I had a dramatic experience of shifting my sense of futility into an awareness of history. I dimly felt I had a mission as a poet for society. A coincidence became my inevitable destiny.

It may appear to be unexpected, but my mental state was converted in that way. The shift was from nihilism to social awareness, from nihilism to historical consciousness.

Prior to that moment, I was completely ignorant about history, nor interested in politics or social issues. Until that moment, I was in a kinship relation, using a distant controller, with the concept of transiency received from ancient India and the unhistorical cycle of life.

After having those experiences, a fierce spirit of protest came to me, and death and nihilism left me. In a day I was out on the street, leading at the forefront of the protesting

TOMORROW

On those tough days of pain
tomorrow was my only honour, like the blue sky.
That was the sole strength I was left with,
as hopelessly I had to wave and
bid farewell to each waning day.

What was really true?
Was it this,
or that?
Or that again?

In the days past,
under the starlight countless nights shot up,
if loving, hating,
and my fatherland
were only things of today,
then leave the glass empty
without offering me any drink.

Although gorgeous flesh and dictatorship are one,
oh, that wretched destiny,
if it is today's,
tomorrow will be already coming, shining,
without receiving any welcoming words,
alone, like a child,
in the wind beyond.
Tomorrow! What a dazzling name!

—from *Fatherland Stars* (1984)

line. I was blacklisted and suffered countless persecutions from the government.

During one period I was under close surveillance by an agent of the KCIA (Korean Central Intelligence Agency), who slept beside me in my room and went to the public bath with me, and attended a wedding ceremony where I was the officiant. There were times when I was under simultaneous surveillance at the same time from the police, from the KCIA and from military security.

In fact, such a change didn't happen solely to me. The death of a worker transformed and awakened a number of intellectuals who had been keeping silent under the military regime.

THREE

POETRY AND JUSTICE

RJ: From 1972 onwards, Ko Un the poet becomes Ko Un the political activist. Ko Un became one of the spokesmen for Korean writers and artists opposed to Korea's dictatorial regimes. How did you relate poetry and politics?

Ko Un: I established a resistance group of writers. I not only served as a spokesperson for that literary group, but I also worked as a key member in the organisation that consolidated dissident movement bodies comprised of religious leaders, intellectuals including academics, and political leaders. It was not because I had a special administrative ability but I had an inexhaustible passion that made me take on that role. Pastor Moon Ik-Hwan and I even considered a prison cell as a blessing.

It was the prison cell that enabled me to experience poetry without poems and to reach a linguistic world of my own, that is, to experience something beyond words in a place where language was strictly forbidden. Prison was also a place for intellectuals to get to know the common people.

Poetry cannot be possible without the real world. But poetry cannot be possible without transcending that reality. These two kinds of impossibilities make poetry come

My Poems

In those years of zero in the ruins of the 1950s
the full-stops scattered here and there after the
 war
were unexpected salvation
for me, rapt wandering.
Because of the sacredness of the black dot after a
 word
the words that followed sometimes shone,
so I wanted to put full-stops constantly in my
 poems.
In the 1970s
my poems, lingering before a long journey
like water swirling by a river bank,
flew out to the centre of the river
in bewilderment.
In the course of time
full-stops disappeared from my poems,
the salvation I had found, like a fully worn-out
 shoe,
becoming null.
Poems without full-stops
did not end as individual poems
but flowed on,
on to other poems.
Pecking at the light hidden from darkness
I could barely see with it things and beyond them.

The world's movement
allowed one full-stop
before my poems.
Consequently

alive between the two worlds, that of reality and the world beyond reality.

I am not sure but I remember that John Bayley, a professor of literature at Oxford University, confirmed that the life of poetry can be found in a heroic self-abnegation confronting the political reality of each country among the poems in each place of the world. It is always part of the nature of poetry that poetry does not remain in simple sentiments, things and minds of the past, but takes protests against power and violence as its theme.

Nonetheless, I strongly reject the dogmatic insistence that political poems are what poetry is all about or more important.

I wrote in the preface of my *Complete Poems* in the early 1980s: 'Poetry is truth at the forefront. Therefore, under any circumstances the avant-garde is poetry.' Those words are still unchanging truth.

However, I also take the starting zero-point of poetry, to which I always return as a baby poet, as the inborn nature of my poems. Poetry is my *samsara*, this world, as well as my *nirvana*, the world beyond. And for a baby, fairy tales and the beginning of imagination are also reality. The world of fairy tales is not real, but to a baby it has an independent reality separate from the reality of its mum and dad. It is the same with poetry.

RJ: And in today's world, do you still think that poets should get engaged politically against injustice and inequality?

KO UN: Injustice and inequality are the challenges and tasks of humanity as it responds to its will to achieve justice and its desire to achieve equality. Injustice and inequality are the oldest vices in the history of mankind. They have repeatedly made our dreams of justice and equality futile.

my poems without full-stops could
be nothing but movements,
that is what I learned.
Apart from that
all perception was illusion.
So I dreamed of the days when
my poems would become other poets' poems
like flocks of birds flying up,
like flocks of birds landing.
Ah, what a range of breathtaking moment
the blue light at dawn is!
But today
flows as a river knowing no fatigue, with endless
  previous days,
and my poems will have no full-stops tomorrow
  and the days after.

—from *A Cenotaph* (1997)

The meaning of justice and freedom is often influenced by power. In our world, truth, freedom or emotion cannot provide the kind of answers mathematics can offer. What is considered justice on one side can be injustice on the other side. Such relativity is the reality of our world.

Poetic universality does not necessarily apply only to the challenges of our reality. As poetry erases the boundary between reality and dream, and then makes the reality dream and dream realises reality once again, this task of transformation is the mission given to poets.

Injustice cannot be overcome in a single day. Inequality has never weakened since the primitive communism of the Old Stone Age. Social hierarchy and discrimination are not simply a matter of politics. They maybe mankind's biological as well as existential destiny. Possession as a human desire has always been the first goal for humankind.

It is an enormous challenge that no revolution or regime in the future can solve. Still, we have another goal without avoiding this problem, as well as a task of controlling our possessions. That is the reason why the meaning of equality can never be deleted from our world.

Maybe my poetry is partly hidden in my hand in the midst of such windstorms. Based on this stark reality I have dedicated one part of my heart enthusiastically to the highest human values such as social justice or equality.

In the real world, the predominant system or ideology often misleads people into biased justice or monopolises justice. In reality, equality is always avoided. It is likely to be floating in the air as an empty concept.

Therefore, we need to stay mentally vigilant, in a state of emergency at all times, to prevent private matters being sacrificed for the sake of public matters, or dedication to public matters being diminished for the sake of private desires.

Equality

Equality is not a matter of making the Earth
and Moon the same size.
It is not the 5-all of our dreams.
A score of 6-to-4 is probably the happiest
equality.

Equality 2

It is a dream.
It is despair.

Justice

Is justice power?
Or is it rather the most powerful dream?

Power

The essence of power is violence.
It hasn't changed since primitive Communism.
Today nuclear, media, internet programs,
culture,
are all powers equal to political power.

I myself would like to keep the public and the private together. My wish is that my true love for my family should be one with my practice of social justice and also my embrace of the universe.

The Earth never stops its movements of revolution and rotation. Revolution would refer to public matters, rotation private. With this combination of private and public matters the universe moves endlessly.

Possession

A sense of possession is stronger in the old.
But nowadays, the young are no different from the old.
They want to have without working. They want to throw away.
Buddhism's non-possession and the non-possession of medieval Christian monks
might be a subject which propagates the meaning of possession to humanity.

Desire 2

It is indispensable.
It is inevitable.
Without it, the world cannot be made.

Revolution

The moment a revolution succeeds it is no longer a revolution.
That is why Ho Chi Minh and Che Guevara are once again revolutionaries.

Socialism

It is tomorrow.

Humanity

A master of one period on Earth.

History

History is a politics of memory and a tomb of
truth.
Dialogue with history is in the end a monologue.
Fortunately, your imagination only prospers in
history.

War

There is no world without war.
There is no world history without war.

Only a defensive war is a holy war.

—from *Forest of Concepts* (2009)

FOUR

POETS AND THEIR IDEALS

RJ: Yet, there are very few poets today who would sign petitions for prisoners or go to prison for their ideals.

KO UN: I won't argue over what other poets believe. Poets have their own characteristics and personalities, and we need to accept and be generous to all.

Even so, poets should have reasons to be willing to go to prison. Only I would like to point out that prison is a specific society and at the same time a place where human beings are structurally destroyed.

It is always the case that we poets and writers have a duty to rescue our fellow writers in various parts of the world who suffer in order to keep his or her conscience, either through International PEN or through international bodies that support imprisoned writers and intellectuals.

I myself also benefited from such rescue movements of writers and intellectuals around the world in the late 1980s and early 1990s. I learned later that Salman Rushdie was also one of those rescued along with me. I also joined the movement advocating for a Palestinian poet under persecution.

RJ: Do you consider poets without social understanding to be ignorant?

A White Sail

No one wants a gale to blow, to sure!
And yet you, white sail out there on the sea,
You yearn for a gale with all your heart:
Because only in a gale
Can you really come alive.

One white sail of endurance and longing,
Far out on the dark blue sea:
Our battle!

I can't tear my eyes away.

Of course, to the grass beneath my feet,
This light mountain breeze must seem a gale!

—from *Fatherland Stars* (1984)

Ko Un: To be frank, there are more poets who are reluctant to engage in social matters. Poets too are fragile human beings vulnerable to fear. I don't despise or disparage them. Who knows, one day we might hear the deep sound of the bell tolling from some of those who have later become involved in social engagement?

It is true that there are not many writers on a par with Sartre and Solzhenitsyn, or Pramoedya, national hero and writer in afflicted Indonesia. Personally I have a greater sense of closeness to the speculative Sartre, rather than Camus who you have worked on. At a time when France had trouble in Algeria, I remember hearing that De Gaulle had responded when a minister suggested arresting Sartre, 'He is another France,' and let him be free. In my opinion, Camus is literature and Sartre is beyond literature.

RJ: Would you say that poetry always survives greater crises? How did you survive the Korean dictatorship as a poet?

Ko Un: In 1979, President Park Chung-Hee's military dictatorship had lasted for nearly two decades. At that time, his number-two man was planning to massacre in one fell swoop around 200 Korean leaders in the various sectors of the democracy movement, similar to the massacres that had taken place in Cambodia. In the meantime, a *coup d'état* occurred and the president as well as his number-two man were assassinated. There were also rumours that the CIA of the US was behind the incident.

It happened when I was in the prison, so I was released. However, in May 1980, the next year, I was imprisoned again for conspiracy of rebellion and received a long prison sentence.

As a poet, I kept courage and was ready to die at any time. Probably that was what gave me the power to survive.

First Person Sorrowful

I am sad. Enlightenment soon becomes a
  contradiction.
After the revolution early last century
the Soviet poets
decided they would only say 'We'.
They decided they would only call themselves
'We'.
They were enchanted.
Their decision held
even when they could not go out into the streets,
even when they lingered indoors
due to heavy blizzards.
They took oaths saying 'We ...'
by themselves.
'I' had disappeared somewhere
deep in the looking-glass.
Mayakovsky, too, one bright sunny day, dashed out
shouting and shouting 'We'.
He was a poet of the street.
'I' was not allowed anywhere.
'I' was wicked.
'We'
'We ...'
That alone had incantatory power.

Little by little, a low-pressure front settled in.
Summer flowers kept being trampled.
Revolution
devoured revolution.
The air went out of every child's ball.

Poetry has gone through many ups and downs with its golden times and its crises through the 10,000 years of its existence and the 5,000 years of its recorded history. There were times when poetry itself was the music of the world and times when it was a sign of curse and fall. Nevertheless, poetry has a fiery magma at its root that makes it always eager to celebrate truth.

Power always wants to make poetry its attendant of adulation and flattery. Poetry has sung paeans for generations of power and war, while on the other hand poems have expressed satire and fury. And at every transitional period in civilisation, poetry has met with crises in which the form of poetry itself became invalidated or extinguished. Poetry has been pushed aside as a thing of 'analogue' in the digital civilisation that started to flourish in the late twentieth century, and perhaps that can be understood in the same context.

From 1934, one year after I was born, 'the death of poetry' was talked about in the West. And this 'death' has since then widened and deepened, until today. Nowadays, even in East Asia, it's common to express 'the end of modern literature'.

When Paul Valéry died in 1945, France mourned his death, giving him a state funeral. Perhaps it might have signified the end of poetry. Nowadays, the death of a poet is no better than death in the street of a sick wayfarer.

Maybe that is due to a huge growth in the number of poets compared to the past, but it is wretched to interpret the death of a poet as the death of poetry. When Byron died from an ailment on the battlefield, fighting for the independence of Greece, his death itself was taken as the climax of poetry. I feel that literature was alive as the top festivity of the world until the twentieth century, but in the twenty-first century, the alienation of literature has grown.

Likewise the taut round atmosphere
of 'We'
slowly went flat.
Someone boldly wrote
'I am in love',
but still, as long the custom,
it was read, 'We are in love'.
Winter snows had not all melted.
Spring is always uncertain.

Late last century
the Soviet Union disappeared.
Countries dropped out of the Warsaw Pact
one after another.

Since then
poets have nothing but 'I'.
Starting with 'I'
they end the day with 'I'.
There is nothing
except 'I'.
God, too, is another name for 'I'.

Today I bury
the ghosts of 'We' and 'I' in the endless waves of
  the Pacific Rim
Who will be born?
Who will be born,
neither 'We' nor 'I'?
Each wave is one wave's grave, another wave's womb.

—from *Belated Songs* (2002)

For example, I have sometimes observed that the poetry festivals and literary festivals held in various parts in the world, although surely there are countries whose poetry festivals are still crowded, have tended to become parties for poets and writers themselves in the twenty-first century.

Wole Soyinka who attended an International Poetry Festival held in Greece, commented that the festival was like a school play. I have sometimes even felt that a poetry festival looked like a memorial ceremony, no longer a festival. Sometimes I felt that a poetry festival is a time when patients with incurable diseases gather to mourn their own writing.

The law of the conservation of mass is much referred to, but I would like to emphasise that quality without quantity is false, that the flowers of quality blossom in the soil of quantity and that quantity is a maternal body for quality. The quality of literature needs to look for a quantity of literature. I am not speaking in high terms of popular literature. When literature disregards the concept of mass, the burden it takes on is an extremely heavy one.

Poetry in the absence of readers and listeners is nothing but a monologue of its writer. In ancient China, when Li Po visited various parts of the land, there were many members of the social elite as well as commoners who were mesmerised by his poems. Writers with no readers may not be writers.

Korea used to be truly a country with a strong tradition in the literary art which was very much admired, and in poetry which was loved a lot. Even in modern times, say, from the 1960s until the 1990s, poetry reigned as the standard for the whole range of culture and arts, much loved by numerous readers. Some poetry books sold several hundred thousand copies. Some of my books, too, were read by tens of thousands of readers and a novel of mine by several hundred thousand people. In the 1980s and 1990s, I was surrounded by poetry lovers.

Today, just like the poetry of many countries in the world, most Korean poetry is shut up in the valley of the poet's introverted ego, rather than being interested in social, historical reality. Sometimes, poems are accompanied by monologues or sensual somnambulism of the senses rather than dialogue. Yet their poetic techniques are superb. Lee Sang, a Korean poet of the 1930s, once wrote that 'despair begets technique'.

Poetry, however, cannot fade away entirely, because poetry is the rhythm of universal phenomena. Both reality and the universe are fields for the poet. What's more, poetry is a super-humanistic custom of the soul. Also, poetry as a life movement is permanently protesting against the contradictions of the age. William Blake's roar like a fierce flame attacking imperialism displays the immortality of poetry.

FIVE

A SENSE OF REALISM

RJ: You always wrote poems despite your intense political activity. Did you continue to write poems when you were imprisoned for a short time?

KO UN: In the past there were several occasions when I decided to give up writing. That was either because of my self-abandoning protest against reality, or my own literary disillusionment. However, after those moments of dejection were over, I found myself working again under the lamp.

I never stopped writing, even during the 1970s and 1980s while I was living on the streets, intensely involved in democratic and human rights movements. I have never been lazy with the job of writing. I had no other choice but to keep writing, because something kept coming to me and was in my way until it got written.

In Korea in the 1970s and 1980s, regardless of his prison term, long or short, the prisoner was not allowed a piece of paper or a pen to use. If I had been given writing instruments behind bars, I believe that I would have achieved something far better than I have done so far. Jawaharlal Nehru wrote *Glimpses of World History* while he was in prison. During President Park Chung-Hee's and

⋆

While I was rowing
I lost the oar.

For the first time I looked round at the wide
  stretch of water.

⋆

In the middle of the road
two dogs are coupling.

I take another route.

⋆

Following the tracks of an animal in the snow
I looked back at my own footprints.

⋆

Soundless!

Resin buried underground is turning into amber
while above the first snow is falling.

⋆

As I was going down
I saw it,
the flower I didn't see as I was going up.

⋆

A thousand drops
hanging from a dead branch.

The rain didn't fall for nothing.

⋆

Heavy snow is falling.
Heavy snow is falling. Everyone is guiltless.

—from *Flowers of a Moment* (2001)

President Chun Doo-Hwan's regimes, they feared above all giving imprisoned poets ball-point pens.

RJ: You have always been a prolific writer. I admire your energy. It looks like writing is an important part of your everyday life.

Ko Un: So far, I have published about 160 books: the count was done by an acquaintance of mine who made my homepage. There is a seven-book epic *Mount Baekdu. The Complete Works by Ko Un* contained in 38 volumes, published in 2002, is almost as tall as I am.

Strangely enough, my poetry collections are getting thicker as I get older. *Maninbo* (*Ten Thousand Lives*), completed in 2010 in 30 books, contains 4,001 poems, and the index shows that 5,600 different names appear. *Untitled Poems* published in 2013 consists of about 690 poems in some 1,000 pages.

Cheong, which is yet to be published, is another big epic, of over 1,000 pages. It is based on a simple oral story and I spent a long time planning and writing with the intention of covering the Asian thought and consciousness, even emulating the representative Western epics, and it encompasses the celestial world, the netherworld and the terrestrial world.

Besides the ordinary poems, long poems and epic poems, I continue to write short poems, which are frequently acclaimed as one of my finest poetic features and accomplishments.

Poems are always coming to me. At times, I copy down the poems I have written in my dream. When poems come to me while I take a walk, I go straight to my study to write them down as soon as I return home, lest I should lose them. Yet there are not a few poems I lost. My day

THE POEM IN LAST NIGHT'S DREAM

Look at the bird
at the edge of its nest.
Look at the bird perch at the edge of its nest
and then flying away.

After the bird has flown
look at the empty nest.
The pure emptiness.
Now look at the gray sky.

—from *The Road Ahead* (1993)

never passes without writing. My wife likes me most when I write and she always supports and encourages me.

RJ: Between 1974 and 1978, you published four collections of poems entitled *In Munui Village*, *Going into the Mountains*, *After Mountain Seclusion* and *Early Morning Road.* Did you feel a change from your first poems?

Ko Un: A number of literary critics consider that the poems up to *In Munui Village*, published in 1974, represent the first half of my poetic production. The poems in these collections were mostly written in the early 1970s. Even though I had already turned to social engagement, my activities were not yet reflected in my poems, and my poems were not separated from the earlier poetics of 'extinction' or 'resignation'.

The intense resolution shown in *Going into the Mountains* (*to Become a Buddhist Monk*) probably reveals the themes of agony and determination I went through while my previous poetical style and way of life were in transition.

Then, by the time *Early Morning Road* was published, my life and poetry became synonymous. As a poet, I entered into the period of my social engagement that would take up over two decades of the middle period of my life.

I suppressed the apriority or unconsciousness in my own poems and the poet's consciousness itself. I entered another state from that which I had been: my consciousness and action arose from my spine, not from my heart, and the physical, linguistic strength grew larger.

I yielded an intensified response to the reality and consciousness of the situations, and my poems naturally responded to and made a sound of heated passion. In that sense, my realism was often strong in the subjectivity of the boiling point rather than the objectivity of the freezing point.

Destruction of Life

Cut off parents, cut off children!
Cut off this and that, and what's not that, too,
and anything else as well
with the blade of knife in the dark.
The next morning
when the whole world is piled with dead things,
our job is to bury them all day long,
and establish there a new world.

—from *In Munui Village* (1974)

SIX

THE ART OF THE NOVEL

RJ: Many people don't know that you are also a novelist. Actually, you wrote many novels in the 1970s, including *Eclipse* and *Little Pilgrim* in 1974, or *A Shattered Name* in 1977, and *The Wandering Souls: Hansan and Seupduk* in 1978. Where did this sudden desire of writing novels come from?

Ko Un: Writing novels is like a relaxation for my conscious self while I work on my main job of writing long and short poems. The prolix style of prose and the long breath of the writing action, compared to the condensation of poetry, were sometimes a fascination in my life.

Then I wrote novels and short stories with narrative content and amount that could be expressed only in novels and short stories. Among them, some were made into movies. *Little Pilgrim*, a boy's Buddhist itinerary, was made into a film that won a special prize at the Berlin Film Festival.

I have covered many different genres, including poetry, criticism, biographies, essays, poems and stories for children, etc. I am a little bit sorry that I haven't had a chance to write a play. Along with writing poems I still write critical reviews as well as keynote speeches on the humanities.

POETRY

All definitions of poetry,
rot!

POETRY 2

The past 5,000 years of poetics and poetic theories
  are all a load of trash.
The meaning of poetry
is just being born, mewling.

POETRY 3

Since I was seventeen,
poetry has been my polar star.
Poetry makes me walk along the road.

—from *Forest of Concepts* (2009)

Nevertheless, I am ultimately only a poet. When I die, I want to die as a poet.

RJ: You consider yourself first and foremost a poet, so do you write novels poetically or do you think as a novelist?

Ko Un: If poetry is dance, fiction can be a movement either prior to or after dance. In Asia, language and music were formerly considered to be undivided, and there was a prehistoric concept that language and dance go together.

In Asia, poetry and dance, dance and poetry, are defined as simultaneous actions, saying 'one sings of one's own accord and one dances of one's own accord'. The French poet Paul Valéry also said that 'poetry is dancing and prose walking'.

I pay attention to the fact that when a novel has poetry in it, its literary aesthetic is heightened. Readers notice that my novel *Little Pilgrim* has not a few poetic elements, because I originally intended to write it as a long epic, but later shifted to the form of a novel. There are dozens of poems in it. That is probably the reason why critics or readers often remark that my novels are highly poetic.

In the case of fiction, the structural arrangement of the plot needs to be concentrated on more than poetic insight and its tissue of inner rhythms. So when I wrote novels and medium-length or short stories, I tried to adhere to their own structures.

Recently I have developed an idea that poetry should be removed from among the genres of literature to be independent and be given a fresh meaning beyond literature. By doing so I want to establish a status for poetry, the oldest heritage of mankind, as a meta-art encompassing the arts in general, and so overcome this age when the novel dominates and there is a flood of non-fiction.

In other words, I would like to draw poetry out of the backwoods into an entirely new dimension and emphasise the broader meaning of poetry, just as poetry was all 5,000 years ago. We can find the possibility of a close affinity between poetry and science, between poetry and philosophy.

SEVEN

THE HOUSE OF BEING

RJ: What is your relationship with language? Do you consider the Korean language as your homeland?

KO UN: Languages are signs of the world, created one phrase after another, in the process of actions from a very long time ago, prior to language itself. Through language the relations within the world, such as that between the subject and the object, were established, and so the object as opposite to the subject was enabled to exist.

Through communication with language the world formulated itself. The signs themselves made our world exist. When philosophers define language loosely as being 'home to existence', that might restrict language to being a repressive structure that is never lenient.

I remember reading that according to the Rig Veda, an ancient Indian collection of Vedic Sanskrit hymns, the languages we use in this world are only one-fourth of the languages of the universe. I have often mentioned for the past 20 years that the words we use on our planet, including my own words, are the 'dialect of the universe'.

I consider that language is the humanisation of rhythms resounding from the infinite emptiness of the universe. I find the origin of poetry in this rhythm of the universe.

I

I was all things in Nature.
I was a ladybird,
a cow,
a red ant,
a yaksa demon,
an oak tree,
and a bug on an oak tree.
I was a beetle,
then, having died,
left my beetle shell in a spider's web swaying in the wind, and set off.
I was a salmon that never returned,
a pond snail,
a poisonous snake in July. The snake's skin was sacred.

I wanted to become a dog
but was the descendant of the most barbarous clansmen in the world.
I was a pedlar
devoured by a tiger.
I was a maggot,
and will be a maggot again.

I
was a hare,
and as a hare
was caught and devoured by a wild boar,
then was born as one of a boar's litter. I disliked wisdom.

It is usually agreed that the Korean language belongs to the Ural-Altaic languages. However, I don't think that Ural-Altaic languages remained without any blood relationship with the ancient Sumerian language or the Indo-European languages.

The origin of the Korean language can be traced from the Scythian horse-riding civilisation. While nomads went wandering in the north, crossing the great mountains and colossal plains and deserts beyond the Urals, Tianshan Mountain as well as the Altai Mountains, and advanced eastwards, their language merged with the far-eastern languages that were close to the Mongolian and Tungus languages. Then once the nomads started to settle down as agrarians, the ancient Korean language was formed.

I now enjoy transnational freedom every full-moon night, as women have their monthly period, that I can reside in any place in the world apart from my fatherland. Then, I bury my patriotic sentiment and fly up into the sky to wander on the jet stream flowing around the world.

More than that, I believe that my destiny as a poet rides on the long-term circulation of the tidal currents of the ocean that occupies most of the surface of the world.

Now I would like to go beyond my fatherland and make the breeze and windstorms of the atmosphere as well as the waves of the ocean my harmony. I want to transcend the obsession with nationalism of modern times.

The horizons on earth and on the sea where humans used to wander for survival are the places of my nostalgia.

RJ: Heidegger says, 'Language is the house of Being.' Would you agree with him that a poet dwells poetically on earth?

Ko Un: I don't want to respond by agreeing or disagreeing with what he said. Heidegger built up the world of his poetic

Born as a human being
I was an awkward shaman,
then my human shape was cast off.
I was an egg broken
before it became a chick,
a goose worn-out from flying day and night, seven
thousand kilometres.
I was an oddjobber in a crossroad tavern in
Cheonan late in the
Goryeo Dynasty,
and a boatman at Buan
in the mid-Yi Dynasty.

I shall be an amoeba. I shall howl and howl on
moonlit nights.

—from *Belated Songs* (2002)

Note: Goryeo Dynasty, 936–1395 AD; Yi Dynasty, 1396–1910 AD.

philosophy or philosophical poetics in his later years when he was isolated due to his cooperation with Nazism, and I find it admirable that he sought self-salvation in such a way. He was blessed to choose poetry and poet at the end of his life, through a profound introspection. Other philosophers would also need to have that kind of blessing.

Now poetry has become a subject to be pursued more by Chinese political leaders, by Gaston Bachelard or Jacques Derrida, than by poets. It has become a phrase of the human spirit inspiring a search for the subject.

The philosophy of the future might be a poetics. The singular point of poetry and philosophy will be found there. The harmony of poetry with science as well as of poetry with technology will be realised as we wish. Then literature as well as philosophy will have their missions in the world together with the brilliant converging capacity of the sciences. Surely a new era of poetry will come.

This world does not solely belong to poets. It is also a dwelling place for thieves and evildoers. The question if a poet dwells poetically on earth should go to Hölderlin or Rilke who lived before me.

For myself, I don't like to make a distinction between poetry and things poetic.

FRONT OF A TREE

Look at the man from the back.
If there were a god
would that be how he looked
on earth?

Even a tree
has a front and a back,
not just because of sunlight,
not just because of north and south.
When I meet a tree in front
and part from its behind
I miss it.

Though the tree can't say a word
when it hears of love
its leaves wave in the breeze.
New leaves next year
will be more dazzlingly green.
No one can stop the turning of leaves at the end
of summer.
No break
between a man and a man
can cut the ties with autumn leaves.
'Stay with us!' they whisper.

—from *Songs of Tomorrow* (1992)

EIGHT

POETRY BEYOND BORDERS

RJ: Would you describe some of your poetry as patriotic?

Ko Un: I dislike very much the concept of patriotic exclusivism. If my praises of Korea should unintentionally lead me to discriminate against or belittle other countries, then I would stop doing it at once. Please let us not talk about things like patriotism, biased nationalism, or the Monroe Doctrine. The reason I took a leading role in the struggle for national unification or a nationalistic view of history in the 1970s through the 1990s was that I believed that I could contribute to making our incomplete history complete, and that it was a creative initiative to make our unification a new type of unification, not a mere reunification.

Our national consciousness at that time aimed at collecting power socially and culturally in order to strengthen the country's resistant capacity against excessive foreign influence and neo-colonialism.

A large number of my poems written in the 1970s and 1980s have a patriotic sentiment in them. After having dedicated myself to the struggle against dictatorship and in favour of labourers' rights in the 1970s, then having lonely and profound experiences of prison life in the early 1980s, I developed an unusually strong concentration of love for

Facing Death

Sea,
When I stand before your three thousand years,

All the inside of my body
will certainly and thoroughly disappear.

I am hungry.
I am hungry.

All that is left is beyond me.

—from *Where Has My Countryside Gone?* (2011)

my country. I wanted to write poems on almost all of my country's nature and environment. I even planned to write about every city and village of my country.

Considering that Vietnam in wartime was the only foreign country I had experienced until then, I had little experience of the outside world and empirically only knew about myself. The title of the poetry collection published in 1984, the first after being released from prison, is *Fatherland Stars*. It was translated into the German and published by Suhrkamp with the same title.

RJ: But, of course, there is a strong sense of belonging in you to the Korean language.

Ko Un: No matter which part of the world I am in, Korean is my one and only language, and King Sejong the Great who invented the Korean alphabet will remain forever my man-god.

Nowadays I am in love with more than one country. If I were to be born again and again in my future life, I would like to move and be born in a different country each time, to create a federal world with those many lives of mine.

As one place is the cause as well as the result of other places, in time too, 12 pm comes before 1 pm, and one is followed by two and then three. In space too, after here is there, and then over there and then again somewhere else.

I, who disdain to be restricted to only one place, am anti-national by nature. The prehistoric nomads' borderless space is my space of liberation. People lived as nomads for millions of years, but have been settlers for less than 10,000 years.

That old DNA of the nomads remains in me as an element of my destiny. I know that an ancient eastern letter depicts a nation as a prison, as a cattleshed. The common people were, in ancient times, blind slaves of the rulers.

From the twenty-first century onwards, I am pleased to be able to share a part of my mind and poetry with foreign countries. Campanella of Italy can be me, Camoes of Portugal my alter ego, and Rumi of Persia my blood relation. Above all, Li Po of ancient China is my big brother, as parentless brothers.

As I feel that there is no border between my consciousness and unconsciousness, I also feel that some part of my consciousness extends to the consciousness of the world. I was born in a place in the Far East, and so I would like to die in a place in the Far West.

A few years ago, the Obama administration of the US made an official announcement that Osama bin Laden's body had been cremated immediately after he was killed and his remains thrown into the Arabian Sea. Nobody knows if it is true or not.

I once wrote that I wanted my tomb to be somewhere in the waves of Pacific Ocean. Even now, I don't mind where my grave is. Borges's grave is not in Argentina but in Switzerland.

NINE

THE IMMEDIACY OF PRESENCE

RJ: Maybe we can repeat here what the American philosopher, Ralph Waldo Emerson, said that a poet can write about the country's noble ideals and achievements, as well as its transgressions. I think you wrote about both?

Ko Un: When I was invited to Harvard University to give a lecture in the early 1990s, I recalled the transcendentalism of Emerson, an alumnus of Harvard University, talking about his drastic shifts to Native American thought or the pantheistic world of India, and praising his bold challenges to the puritan society of North America and his wide view that embraces even Buddhist philosophy. His poetic theory and his outlook on the world were flames in the environment that could be very dangerous for his age. I think it was natural that Thoreau was beside him.

I think I have done with my poems a part of the dual role poetry has for the poet's native land. I think that probably my poems have contributed a little to the duality and totality of life and culture that we should be endowed with basically.

Whatever I write in my poems cannot but be related to my country and encompass both sides of it. In *Maninbo*, for example, there are not a few poems portraying both the beauty and the ugliness of my country.

WHERE HAS MY COUNTRYSIDE GONE?

It's wrong, wrong, wrong.

All of the Korean peninsula is turning into Seoul.
Oh shit, a country with a crush on glitz,
on thousands of flashy *events*.
You, and I,
all of us, ditto,
are turning into New York.
We're turning into that wretched 'hub' or dub of a hub.
I say:
We're turning into the ugliest, most shameless
so-called 'centre'.

The place where once we knew sorrow.
The place that was far from anywhere.
The place we could not leave.
The place we finally left
after being held back,
held back.
The mud-flat of my heart.
That place where, at sunset, we could see clearly
the biennial bloom of quince flowers.

The place that looked the same ten years before
and ten years after.
The place where we lived together
with great-grandmother whom I never once saw,
and great-grandfather, too, whom I never saw,
both there in mother's blurred mirror-stand.
The place where children never felt that
their father's generation was ancient history.
The place where an uneducated father
ploughed an ancient field at dusk.

I want to subordinate myself neither to Korea's old traditions of the taste for the arts that combined Confucianism, Buddhism and Taoism, nor to Buddhism with its 1,600-year-old tradition, nor to Confucianism that served as the national ideology for 500 years.

And when it comes to blind obedience to the modernisation of Korea that came in tardily, I would rather be a primitive radical who broke with it, shouting 'Overthrow modern civilisation!'

However, I might inevitably be an illegitimate child of modern times and a vestige of the ancient times. Often I don't clearly know what kind of person I am.

RJ: Where would you place Korean poetry in the new Korean society?

KO UN: Korea is the Korea of tomorrow. Korea should go beyond the contradiction in which regimes divided as the result of passivity confront each other as enemies, and become a consolidated society.

I yearn for the Korean peninsula to be 'a monism, in other words a pluralism', to become not a single solid entity but a multi-regional republic, governed in harmony, a basic unit of the East Asian communities that can dissolve the nationalistic tensions along the boundaries of East Asia. Thus, Korea will have a new *raison d'être*.

Perhaps Korean poetry will, in that future time, contribute to the dreaming society ranging between nature and technology. The present-yet-to-come is the flower of the many present times that have gone. I wish that Korean poetry finds its direction in this futuristic hope. So far Korean poetry has been more passive than active in this age.

RJ: Are you read by the young Koreans?

The place where truth kept to itself within a
 village.
The place where you fell asleep when I fell asleep.
The place where the uncle we believed dead came
 back alive.
The place where the land-rent was a
 bone-breaking seven-parts-to-three.
The place where people died closing their eyes,
 having no
strength to keep them open.
The place where people with low noses and high
 cheek-bones,
enduring harsh poverty, bowed to the dead on
 ritual nights.
The place where long-term plans were ineffective.
The place where people would gather together on
 rainy days.
The place where, if one died, all mourned.
The place where Kim was an uncle to Jang,
where A and B were cousins.
The place where people like Sir Magistrate never
 appeared.
The place where, on huge full-moon nights,
someone sharpened a kitchen knife
and slashed it gleaming through the air.
The place where meaning bowed down before
 meaninglessness.
The place we have left behind.

Where has my countryside gone?

—from *Where Has My Countryside Gone?* (2011)

KO UN: I hear that there are young people who seek out and read my poems. As far as I know, most of my poetry books are still in print; a few are out of print.

Even so, quite naturally, I might not be a familiar name any longer among those in their twenties and thirties. Far less, I think I might not be as passionately received as I used to be.

Now is the time of the anti-humanities, of pragmatism, of the culture of consumerism and of the internet. Although it is just for a time, now is the time when the digital is in full swing and falsehood is dominant.

However, in any age, the young generation has its own cultural experiences that it should cope with, and also have the right to enjoy them. For the young people have their own idols, their own tastes and the poems they sympathise with easily.

We should admit that for those young people who are used to texting and writing on Twitter, it would not be easy to read something with difficult content that require profound and delicate thinking.

I anticipate that by around 2050 young people will crave the old expressive forms of poetry as a reverse phenomenon of civilisation. It's because the basic nostalgia of humanity is a nuclear matter of the heart, that could be forgotten but will not disappear. Recently, I heard that on the Berkeley campus in the US, serious philosophy is returning. The cutting edge of civilisation ruminates, as a reaction, the memories of civilisation and sometimes returns to them although in different way.

The world consists of the contradictions of gravity, with action and reaction. Just like silence and language.

RJ: Where does the truth of poetry reside: in the immediacy of the presence or in the memory of the eternal?

North Korea

Until when
until when
will you
be my present tense?

Tonight again I shake violently from the
aftershocks of a century of quakes.

—from *Full of Shyness* (2006)

White Butterfly

Behold.
One white butterfly
ghost of wisdom, is flying
over the foolish sea.
All this world's books are closed.

—from *Full of Shyness* (2006)

Ko Un: The charms of 'immediacy of presence' and of 'memory of the eternal' are both elements that poetry cannot lose. One is philosophy, the other religion.

The 'philosophy' and 'religion' we are talking about here should create values with new meaning in the future. As long as poetry is not subordinate to philosophy and poetry is not confined to being an instrument of religion, then the meaning of philosophy in relation with poetry would be a new one.

Also, religion would be a variation as an element in harmony with poetry. J. M. Murray even placed poetry above god. Then poetry will be embodied in both at the same time.

I Write in the Air

I let my ridiculous white pages fly away.
I write with my body alone,
with my soul alone.
I write in the empty sky.

Now I abandon my letters
and shout up at the empty sky.
I rage in near frenzy
at the empty sky.

Now I bury all my junk.
I ascend into the empty sky and dance.

O, that unreachable space beyond
the empty sky!

So-called Father,
so-called Mother,
so-called ancient Great Jade Emperor,
none can assume the name of the empty sky.
Gods
that have not been abolished for millennia,
gods still hovering,
and whatever else may hang around us,
in whatever state,
none can assume that name.

Now, swept away to uninhabited plains,
I repent to the empty sky
with a sobbing so inadequate ...

How far I have roamed to reach this point!
Here at last,

I write a line, bowing my head to all the ages of
empty sky.
I write, well, something.

—from *Empty Sky* (2008)

PART III

A Poet Beyond Self

ONE

DISILLUSIONS

RJ: I read somewhere that you said: 'The poems which I write today make me happier than the poems I wrote yesterday.' What is it like writing poetry as a monk? How can one be a monk-poet?

KO UN: My act of writing poems as a monk was nothing but a way of following the tradition that Buddhist monks of many generations had followed, composing one or two cough-like, condensed, short poems or letters, recording brief images, which are the expression of their core intuitions at the end of long practise during which they refrained from writing to an extreme degree.

In those days I wanted to be a Seon monk more than a poet. When I made my official debut as a poet in 1958, I said that I longed for the fascination of leaving behind a few Buddhist verses or a few letters, like a bird's footprints impressed on the snow, and that would be my only remaining trace. It was only much later that I became aware of the shift of my mind from being a monk to being a poet.

About two years after becoming a monk-poet, I was suddenly at a crossroads. Around the time of the April Revolution in 1960, I was the head of Jeondeung-sa Temple

Echo

To mountain at dusk:
What are you?
What are you are you are you ....

Beyond

Without you
how can I possibly live?

A Drunkard

I've never been an individual entity.
Sixty trillion cells!
I'm a living collectivity.
I'm staggering zigzag along,
sixty trillion cells, all drunk!

A Friend

Hey! With the clay you dug out
I fashioned a Buddha.
It rained.
The Buddha turned back into clay.

Pointless as clear skies after rain.

in Ganghwa Island in the west just below the Korean armistice line.

One day, I climbed to the top of Mount Mani and stayed up all night making a choice between religion and art. I chose literature, which led me to return to the secular world. Since then I have had nothing but poetry.

The reason the poem I wrote today makes me happiest is maybe because I appreciate the 'beginning of life' in which I always become another me. The poem I wrote yesterday is already a memory and belongs to the past. Or rather, it becomes a different world.

I consider it to be futile to divide time into the past, present and future. The past is already gone and so does not exist, and the present too quickly becomes the past. The future is nothing, it is yet to come. That is my theory of timelessness, which is consistent with ancient Buddhism as well as *Confessions of Augustine* in ancient times. Our lives bank on such a river bed of illusion.

When a poem comes, whatever it is, I am conscious of 'its beginning', the very 'moment' of its beginning. Whether from nothingness or not, from some vague foreboding, or from linguistic formation by precise structures, as Edgar Allan Poe claims, I realise that the moment of a poem's birth is the beginning of the universe. The poem in that moment, therefore, is 'the first poem'. The poet draws one hot, gleaming grain, a single word, from the Big Bang of language.

The poem I have just written exhilarates me most. In fact, in my late teens, poetry captivated me physically, even without me knowing what poetry writing was. I confess I still have many such moments.

RJ: Did you ever criticise your own poems or destroy them?

The Pole Star

If you vanished
the north would vanish
the south would vanish
east and west would vanish.
No.

Moon

The bow taut.
Twang!
The arrow strikes your eye.

By the pain of your darkness the moon rose.

Ripples

Look! Do all the ripples move
because one ripple starts to move?
No.
It's just that all the ripples move at once.

Everything's gone greatly askew from the start.

KO UN: In the early 1960s, I burned my unpublished poems and all my books, including my first poetry collection and my first novel. I did it because of the sense of despair I felt after reading Sholokhov's *And Quiet Flows the Don* in utter secrecy, in the shadow of Korea's brutal Anti-communist Law and National Security Law.

With an exaggerated sense of self-negation, feeling that my writing was not true writing, I felt that I was standing on the edge of a precipice. So one night I piled up my manuscripts and books and burnt them all. I was reported as an arsonist and taken to a police station, but I was released with a warning.

After this incident there were several occasions when I decided to stop writing. It was also because of the disillusionment that I had with my poems. Incidentally, one of my essay books published much later is entitled *For Disillusionment*.

This repeated self-hate might have stimulated the poetic urges and the paradoxical patience in order to sustain my own world.

My life as a poet was a life spent embracing poems by pushing them. Absurdly, I might have continued writing poems as a result rather than a cause.

A Single Word

Too late.

The world had already heard
my word
before I spoke it.
The worm had heard.
The worm dribbled a cry.

—from *What!* (1991)

Self Portrait

The song I sang,
the song I couldn't sing
come crashing down on me.

Is it me?
—running with the torch light?
Is it me?
—this luminous regret?

—from *A Cenotaph* (1997)

TWO

THE AVATAR

RJ: Many people around the world write poetry when they are melancholic or in love. But I think your relationship with poetry is different. It seems to me that for you, poetry is an eternal element. You even say that your death will be a poem.

Ko Un: Generally, the world's love poems are written after the loss of love. The failure and loss of love in reality is commemorated, mourned and completed through poetry. This fact is often revealed in many poets' autobiographies and biographies.

Beatrice, celebrated by Dante, became another person's wife. But in *La Divina Commedia*, she is described as an angel of ultimate redemption and sublimated as a sacred and inviolable being who guarantees glory to the protagonist of the oeuvre who is also Dante himself.

As you point out, I think my poems exist as an 'eternal element' in the infinite and unconscious cycle of life. As far as poetry is concerned, I dream of a different world through poetry. I feel vain and bored, being in the valley of this single life, so I lean towards the rich valleys of my previous lives and those of my next and sing about them.

THE WHISPER

Rain falls.
I sit at my desk.
The desk speaks softly:
Once I was a flower, was a leaf, was a stalk.
I was a long root beneath the ground
stretching as far as yon desert oasis.

A scrap of iron on the desk speaks:
I was the uvula of a stillness howling alone on
moonlit nights.

The rain stops.
I go outside.
Grass, thoroughly soaked, speaks to me:
Once I was your joy and sorrow.
I was your history and songs.

Now I speak
to desk
to iron
to earth:
Once I was you, was you, was you.
Now I am you, I am you.

—from *Empty Sky* (2008)

Past life and next life live as realities in the minds of those who dream of them. Today is the immediate descendent of yesterday and the immediate ancestor of tomorrow. On a human time scale, 1 pm comes between 12 am and 2 pm. Likewise, the orphan of this present life is the legitimate child of the previous life and also the parent of the next life.

But I also think that when we condense life in the present world into one single life, we grow more intense in our life and art. It is because the only life is the epitome of countless lives. There is no power as powerful as one single 'once' of the instant that risks death.

RJ: Do you believe in reincarnation? Could you be the avatar of a previous Korean poet?

KO UN: Ancient India and modern India are the same because the carts of the fourth century BC continue to be seen today in the landscape of remote farm villages of Bihar province in India. There, people's names from thousands of years ago are still used today. The name of an Indian woman poet I met at an international poetry festival was Suzata. I was touched by her name because it was also the name of a woman at the time of Buddha.

In Asia, the desire for reincarnation lies in the depths of society. Also, Siberian or East Asian shamanism hints at such schemas of reincarnation. Yet, regardless of the prospect of reincarnation, I fervently long for my poetry to lie alongside me, even as bones and ashes after death.

I regard death as a perfect poem. How can the silence of returning to nothingness, discarding all the superfluity of multiple lives, not be the completion we arrive at in the course of splendid rhetoric and various metaphors?

However, even when 'I' am alive, life and death constantly repeat themselves inside me, as the meetings and partings of material substances. Also, the meetings and partings of the things which constituted me before I became 'I' through my parents, and then death, again with the meeting and partings of material substances, would scatter me into a different I or something else.

Therefore, nothingness is not just nothingness but something else. This terrifying fact creates the wonder of physics, with the maximum of the universe and the basic particles, and poetics as one.

THREE

THE KAMIKAZE

RJ: Talking about previous Korean poets, how do you distinguish your works from those of other modern Korean poets from the past 50 years such as Shin Dong-yeop or Ku Sang?

Ko Un: I have never distinguished nor compared my seniors' or colleagues' poems with mine. It's not because I'm overly humble or overly arrogant. I am constitutionally indifferent to the concept of comparative literature.

And I do not want to settle into the framework of the history of poetry. Pumpkin, Chinese cabbage and watermelon are each and every finished products.

The better you know a poet's face, the farther you get from the poet's poems. So I doubly enjoy the pleasure of meeting poems and poets through the posthumous works of dead poets, past poets, and distant poets. It is the spatial privilege of literature.

There is a theory that the poem cannot be separated from the poet and the trajectory of the poet's life leads the reader to read and understand more of his or her poems. On the other side, there is also a theory that the poet should be excluded from his or her poems. There is also a theory

Freedom

Freedom is a modulation of freedom.

Freedom 2

Poets are unnecessary in freedom.
Those who have never fought for freedom have no
life.

History

History is a politics of memory and a tomb of
truth.
Dialogue with history is in the end a monologue.
Fortunately, your imagination only prospers in
history.

The Avant-garde

There is youth in the avant-garde.
The avant-garde is beautiful because it is defeated.
After that defeat comes a new age.
The avant-garde is not only killed from without,
it is an eggshell being broken from within.

Justice

Is justice power?
Or is it rather the most powerful dream?

—from *Forest of Concepts* (2009)

that emphasises the reader, and not the poet, which is essentially about the dimension of the readers.

In any case, poetry expands its world further through the novelty that comes from the past or the future, which is yet to come. Therefore, you may find yourself more familiar with my poems if you delete me from them.

RJ: Reading some of your poems, I have the feeling that they suggest an immediate heroic context of resistance in a crisis.

KO UN: Indeed, during the early 1970s through early 1990s, part of my poetry often had a heroic tone. It is more than once when my poems contained an attitude of the imperatives. I was often caught by overwhelming emotions as if lightning and thunder swept over me.

It was often the case even in my everyday life. For example, one day while I was drinking with a leading dissident journalist, drunk, I suggested that we commit suicide by burning or disembowelment, or by whatever other means, and we ended up quarrelling outrageously. That journalist mocked me, comparing me to 'a Kamikaze', those Japanese pilots who deliberately committed suicide by crashing their fighter plane into US battleships at the end of World War II.

When this kind of reckless tension was reflected in my poems, it even grew into something very inflammatory. And given that the social atmosphere responded hotly to it, it seems that such poems were necessary at that time.

In the confrontation of literary theories during the China–Soviet Union dispute, Chinese communist literary theory, as a counter-theory opposing the Soviet Union's socialist realism, claimed 'revolutionary romanticism'.

This revolutionary romanticism may have had blood-ties with me. So I insisted that even my friends' realism was

The Road Not Yet Taken

I will not say I've arrived.
Though it's been thousands of miles,
the road to go is longer than the road I've come.
When a day's end comes on the way
and I spend the night like a sleeping beast,
the road to go still far lies ahead.
Though loneliness has been my company,
it wasn't loneliness alone,
it was truly the world.
And the road not yet taken,
it will be surely the world unknown to anyone.
The wind is rising.

—from *Poetry Left Behind* (2002)

a still-life painting and that literature in motion must lay in active romanticism.

And I secretly put my own literary beliefs in *praxis*, practice. For this reason, I gave the name *Practice and Literature* to the 'Mook' magazine I founded, advocating 'practice' instead of 'freedom', which was the value our first writers' movement pursued.

That quarterly magazine is still being published and has evolved into a publishing house called 'Practice and Literature Publishing Company'. The house is now run by the younger generation, my junior friends.

I called this revolutionary romanticism 'historical romanticism'. Here the meaning of the word 'history' was not the concept of 'history of all times and all regions', but that of the avant-garde of modern history.

However, besides these engaged poems, I never neglected even the sound of the lyrical essence found in the universe transcending reality or in the delicate microbial action inside me.

In addition, the free embodiment of Buddhism was also established as a common feature in the unconsciousness of my poems.

By nature, I can't just take one single path in my art. In literature, the singular in one single path is not my world. I still prefer the lure of roving around at three-way or five-way intersections.

Some critics have referred to me as 'the Ko Uns' in view of the multiple categories and great quantity of my literary production, which is probably not irrelevant to this fact.

FOUR

POETRY AND HISTORICAL MEMORY

RJ: When one reads your poem 'Arrows', does one immediately realise Korea's long history of pain?

Ko Un: 'Arrows' is an impromptu poem that was written in the middle of the 1970s from a resolute and tragic sense emerging in a drunken state in the middle of the night. At that time, I was living a life of torrents and passions. This poem was recited and sung in colleges and during many demonstrations for a long time. It was often recited at drinking parties as well.

It contains a youthful and fierce message that only dedication and self-sacrifice can contribute to the history. Due to the sentiment of anti-dictatorship of the time, it received a lot of responses and is often mentioned as a symbol of the 1970s.

But I refuse to accept that any one poem becomes my major work. A representative work is a kind of bureaucratic formality. This descriptive distinction that some poems are more representative than others can make literature dangerously formulaic through schematisation.

RJ: Do you consider yourself an 'arrow' in the context of Korean history?

Arrows

Transformed into arrows
let's all go, body and soul!
Piercing the air
let's go, body and soul.
Let's go and not return.
Transfixed,
rotting with the pain of striking home,
never to return.

Let's all stop breathing and quit the string.
Throwing away like rags
all we've had for decades
all we've enjoyed for decades
all we've piled up for decades,
happiness, the lot.
As arrows
let's all go, body and soul.

The air is shouting!
Piercing the air
let's go, body and soul!
In the dark daylight the target is rushing towards us.
Finally, when the target topples in a shower of
  blood,
all just once
let's bleed as arrows.

Never to return!
Never to return!

Hail, arrows, soldiers of justice and spirits of the
  fallen.

—from *Early Morning Road* (1978)

KO UN: I guess not a few people remember me as such. I was at the forefront at the time of a harsh military dictatorship that is unimaginable now, so I suffered a lot. But I never broke my will in the face of appeasement and suffering.

It seems that, at that time, many people as well as my colleagues and young people were proud of that. I sensed it through the recollections of young people at the time who breathlessly watched and tried to emulate each of my fearless and unhesitating moves. 'Arrows' may have been a fight-urging poem for me.

In the latter days of Park Chung-Hee's military regime, I was offered a chance to be a minister and advised to study either in Paris, France, for five years or in Japan for a long period.

Of course, even after democratisation, I received proposals from the government for key positions such as party vice-president and a proportional representative. Each time, deeming such positions to be unsuitable for me, I flatly refused them.

I have no *raison d'être* other than to be a poet.

RJ: Do you feel that poets are also prisoners of history? How can a poet transcend history with his/her poetry?

KO UN: I don't want to be a bird locked in the cage of Korean history. Whether it is history or reality, I always refuse and take precautions that neither history nor reality become handcuffs that bind the freedom of my fate. I take it to be my literary duty to comfort not just the arrows that hit the target, but also those that miss the target.

In an interview with *The New York Times* in the 1980s, I emphasised that poetry is the music of history. At the time, my poems were all about social reality and the shifts of history.

Pride

Today there is no temple, no ancestral shrine for
me.
I believe in nothing.
With all my bones
I resist the neon signs in the night streets.
Ancestors' arrowheads are still quivering.

—from *Full of Shyness* (2006)

The Rest of My Life

I dare confess:
I am not an orphan inside this country.
I am a missing child out there in the Infinite.

Yes, indeed.
Yes, indeed.

The Infinite!

Without this vast blank page of infinite potential
I would suffocate, unable to live a single day, not
even half a day.
It is not greed.
It is not avarice.
It is acutely the far-off last extremity behind
reality.

—from *Empty Sky* (2008)

However, after our country ended military regimes in the early 1990s and, though incompletely, achieved democratisation, I started to move away from the logic of history and take a stroll or swim around in the internal world of human beings and the universe.

In fact, I do not know what other poetry world I am headed for. Sometimes the journey of a narrative, description or metaphor falls off the road and meets a sudden, unexpected cliff, being cut off and unable to advance.

In short, not only life but also death is the subject of my poems. But you always have to watch out in writing for the theme not to take control of the subject. The thesis in a given period can become a fossil once that period has passed by.

In a lifetime, we encounter several crystals of different meanings. The rosin that falls on the ground becomes amber underground. Pearls are sometimes made in shells.

Life has momentums and opportunities, from which the next comes.

RJ: Do you think your poetry has helped Koreans overcome their painful history?

Ko Un: The days when I lived publicly became an indelible memory for me and are now an indelible record of history. I am honoured that my poems are often quoted in some parts of Korea's modern history.

Basically, I am one of many poets, and my poetry has both public and private areas. If my poems are embellished with too much public significance, it would be a hollow response. Therefore, I want to be arrogant to my heart's content like Nietzsche and then be humble at this point.

Sometimes I also want to wander anonymously through the air of history.

Boiling and evaporation belong to me all.

Request

How many
a branch
a branch
there still must be
on which no bird has ever perched.

Do not say I'm lonesome, lonesome.

Where could there be
a branch
a branch
that has never been shaken by the wind?

Do not say I'm
in pain, in pain.

—from *Where Has My Countryside Gone?* (2011)

RJ: I don't think the pain is over, but can't Korean poets relate to it any longer?

Ko Un: Pain is not limited to a rite at the passages of time. It is a permanent concept. As soon as one pain is overcome, another pain makes its face appear. The Buddha's understanding of the world as a place of pain is one level above understanding it as a place of 'sin'. Pain is a condition of life.

Today, Korean poets generally do not seem to feel, apart from the stress from their existence, any pain, nor do they show any deep thought and insight about pain, whether it be about problems of life, society or history. They seem to be more preoccupied with the ability to express themselves through the language by which they catch themselves.

FIVE

POETRY AND THE SELF

RJ: How do you relate poetry with the rhythms of life? Does poetry precede life by shaping it?

Ko Un: Maybe the act of looking for life's rhythms of self within the forest of selves, according to the changing circumstances, after putting the focus of poetry on the things of reality and the world, raises issues about the public and the private, discussed in social ethics.

But I disregard the long-standing practice by which the public is a super-ordinate concept of the private, and the private a part or an object of the public. I understand them as simultaneous and equal.

Furthermore, these two are different but identical phenomena. The rotation and revolution of a planet happen on the level of a kind of cosmic public and private, in order to keep the planet moving permanently.

It is true that in current civilisation, as time goes by, poetry becomes distant from history, social consciousness and community perception. The switch from social necessity to literary choice is a phenomenon of twenty first–century literature.

Perhaps today's poetry is conducting a nuclear test, pursuing its own form in a different civilisation, preceded by

Some Advice

Poems
block the path for better poems.
Poems
block the path for subsequent poems.

Poems, poems, my blue poems!

Escape somehow from the history of poetry,
from fashions of poetry,
from a hundred years of poetic authority.

Be born trembling, wild and alone.

—from *Empty Sky* (2008)

the nomadic and agricultural ages, as well as the primary, secondary and tertiary industrial ages.

It is clear that poetry will be in the reality of a different dimension beyond that located on earth, or in the reality of a particular region.

Poetry has sometimes preceded the times, but it also follows the times.

RJ: Do you think that the self-centered way of experiencing life is killing poetic imagination?

Ko Un: It is the reality of the world that the active tries to fulfil the desire to reject and control the passive, the subject, the object, and the self, others.

I used to abuse and hate myself to the level of making it an illness, and when the time came that I hated even this habit, I came to a state of mutated self-affirmation, especially in my twenties and thirties. Once in a while when it was dissolved by the thought of selflessness, the sense of the euphoria of the equilibrium was close to ecstasy.

The speaker in a poem is a reflection of myself as well as of an unknown, an imaginary self. After all, my life and experience in this world stay within the boundaries of 'I', so those times in my life path form some limits that contribute to my poetry.

Life is a reality that can expel poetry, but it is also composed of the elements of a periodic table of dreams that constantly evokes poetry.

'Poetry is experience.' 'Poetry is impossible when it is away from life.' These basic theories of poetry have often been mentioned in the poetical circles of every part of the world, not just in ancient times but even in the twentieth century.

Then the infinity of poetic liberation opens up, which was completely different from the level of experience, such

Monologue

The lonesome communist José Saramago once
 said that
joy and sorrow,
go together
because they are not water and oil.
I nod.
Nod.

Then I object:

Joy knows no sorrow.
Sorrow knows no joy.

I refuse sudden enlightenment.
All the dialogues in the world, frogs' night-long
 choruses,
ultimately they're each a monologue.
Flowers and sudden frosts on spring flowers,
each a monologue
to the very end.

What is truly amazing
is that dialogue
has never existed in this world of greed and lust,
no, not even once.
To the end, each and every aloneness
is so hard-shelled it has no sense
of having ever been alone.

—from *Where Has My Countryside Gone?* (2011)

as Bachelard's imagination of water and fire. In some cases, even memory was possible within the imaginary world.

Nowadays this kind of imagination is turning into an excessively mechanical force in the endless adventure of the digital world. Under such circumstances, I am instinctively on the watch for phenomenon where the way of experiencing life becomes conventional and only imagination can be absolute.

In my case, my poetry exercises its veto over my own restrictions. This is because the empowerment of an image, often likely to be illusory, manifests itself as the fury of crisis in reality. In this case the image can be also a crime.

RJ: How can one be a poet with a sense of no-self?

KO UN: Two years ago, I made a long keynote speech about self and selflessness at an international literary festival. The other panel members sympathised with my speech. In short, what I said was that just as spring blossoms turn into autumn leaves and fruits, the ego is transformed into a completely different world before one knows it.

The nothingness of the world is not non-being as the counterpart of being, but a void that encompasses both being and non-being. In this void, the world spreads a net of endless relations and in this process, the fixed concept called the self cannot be permanently guaranteed anywhere. I think that the quantum mechanics of the multi-universe theory perhaps corresponds to this.

In fact, from a very long time ago, probably since the late twentieth century, many poets have made cocoons of 'I' and 'self', the subject of modern times, and have lived inside them.

Most poets have lived a fixed life of prejudice and subjectivity centring on 'I' and 'self', to the extent that they

A Reply

Child,
that
isn't a flower.
That isn't a butterfly.

They are nothing but shadows.
I am
too,
and from long ago.

What should you do? What should I do?

—from *Where Has My Countryside Gone?* (2011)

themselves came to abhor it. They are imprisoned in the illusion that there is 'I' and that this 'I' is immortal.

I know intuitively the empty space left behind after the vanishing of ancient nomadic nations, my poetry's domicile of origin. Otherwise, I will give up being a poet.

SIX

POETRY IN KOREA

RJ: Is poetry still popular in Korea? Are Koreans still a people of poetry?

Ko Un: Korea has long been known as 'the country of poetry'. Literature and poetry were respected, and the social and cultural influence of poetry was great. And poets, too, were loved and respected. People read a lot of poems, and everyone quoted them frequently.

There was a dominant view that Korea fell victim to Japanese imperialism by the fact that the martial culture of Japan's samurai had overthrown the literary arts of Joseon's scholars.

Now we live in the norm of the trends of another civilisation and culture. Even today, when people don't read serious poems much, due to the advent of demographic decline and the rapid increase of other entertainment interests, in Korea, as if going against the age, the number of poets has increased to tens of thousands, disregarding their quality.

Some days, I receive three or four newly published poetry books as gifts. I am not sure whether I can confirm that Koreans still enjoy reading poems because of this unusual phenomenon. As in other countries, poetry has

Moonlit Night

This is tonight fifteen hundred years ago.

The moon on its path, bewitched
by some plaintive flute sounds,
listens attentively to the world below,
listens to its heart's content,
then moves on.

The flute ceases before a soul knows
that the moon has quite set.

No enemies anywhere.

—from *Empty Sky* (2008)

been changing to more inward expressions since the twenty-first century.

Koreans of today are like an army of the information civilisation. The alienation of poetry lies undeniably behind the global leadership of Korea in information technology.

If my mistaken prophecy ever comes true, we will once again become a people of poetry decades later at the earliest. For now, digital fanaticism centred on the internet, rising like the sunrise, is completely dominant.

The wistful moonlit night celebrated by an ancient Korean song 'Song from Jeongeup', or the calm communion in such a night with family members who were in the faraway world of the dead, was linked to the present until recently.

But now such an imagination is not valid at all. Worse than that, in contemporary civilisation, people reveal vulgar and wicked human instincts more often and more straightforwardly.

Nonetheless, there is always a distant past somewhere in any *dernier cri*.

RJ: Is *sasolsijo*, the traditional three-line free-form narrative poetry, still practised among the Korean people? (Do you write such poems?)

KO UN: The freewheeling prose of sasolsijo emerged in the later period of feudalism, rejecting the standards and the legitimacy of logical conclusions that the Yangban class and the ruling culture made, and also attempted to venture into non-grammatical and non-ethical freedom.

In Korea, *sijo* (traditional Korean poem with a fixed form, composed of three verses for one stanza) are still constantly written and sometimes recommended; there are numerous professional sijo poets. However, although the fixed-form sijo is still written a lot, the whole idea of sasolsijo has disappeared and is often performed as a traditional form

7 Short Poems

★

A cold wind
stirs
the yellow feathers of the baby chicks.
Chicks' legs stay thin for a long time.

★

A thump!
like the sound of a huge rock being dropped.
Was it a sound made by the darkening mountain?
After,
the owl's eyes became bigger.

★

In the stable where to the bitter end a sick horse
  refused to kneel down
a faint light of dawn is spreading.
It was a long night,
a long, long night.

★

Do I have the love of one person
that can wash away the hatred of several people?
I had been opening an umbrella,
but I closed it again,
and just welcomed the rain.

★

I asked a child:
Do you want to be a beggar,
or a thief?
The child asked:
Why, is there nothing
but that in this world?

like *pansori* (traditional Korean narrative recital by a single person of a dramatic story of several characters).

By nature, I dislike standard forms and repetition, so that the poetics of sijo literature, with its orderly logical development of introduction-development-turn-conclusion, does not constitutionally suit me.

Therefore, I prefer the freedom of short poems that go beyond formality to sijo form. Perhaps this poetic inclination is connected to the world of Buddhist Seon that I am familiar with.

I have published several collections of short poems, including a collection of Seon poems, *What?* (1991). My short poetry collections seem to be still much loved. *Flowers of a Moment* (2001) is known to have sold about 100,000 copies.

Gary Snyder, an American poet, once pointed out that my short poems show a world that is different from the epigrams of ancient Greece and Japanese haiku. I was reported that my Seon poetry collection was reprinted several times in the United States.

The reason why short poetry collections are read a lot may be reflected partly on the fact that people have less time to enjoy reading long poems, and that their taste has become more fragmentary.

I no longer want to apply the words 'intuition' or 'inspiration' to my poetry, as people often do, when talking about the way I continuously write short poems. Perhaps the ebullition of my short poems is an algebra, natural and raw.

RJ: It is interesting how your poetry has always been close to the narrative of the Korean people.

Indeed so. In this world, there is only the Caspian
Sea and the
Black Sea.
★
Let go
of the things you have spent thirty years shouting
for.
Among them,
justice!
Let go of it forever.
★
Today
may be a trivial day,
the day someone is being born,
someone is leaving,
someone waiting.
Today too, the glow of the setting sun is glorious!

—from *Poetry Left Behind* (2002)

KO UN: I am not sure. Narrative expression is an innate ability and, more than that, an ability that one meets on all the roads of the world.

My blood surely touches the narrative expression of the Korean people. If so, my veins are surely to be connected to the faraway lands that Koreans came across long ago, so I often feel the identity of my poetic veins with the Huns or with Scythians.

It would be natural that my poems are very friendly to the Korean narrative because I am a poet who loves *hangeul*, the Korean alphabet, and has long written in hangeul.

Also, I love to borrow and use a lot of ordinary, popular expressions, not special poetic diction or expressions, and so my writing is probably closer to Korean ways of expression.

However, if I'm an Aborigine in Australia, the sound of their all-night drumming will be sure to resound in my poems. Just as the wind ignores races and borders, some of my narratives will resonate the expressions of ten thousand years later as well as of ten thousand years ago in the blank pages as the sound of their wind.

Toyohara

Toyohara, who lived outside of Seomun, was a cripple.
When he came home after slogging over the pass outside Seomun
and the pass in Okjeong-gol,
the hills swayed nicely,
the sky too.
When he reached Soijeongji
the local elders who had finished their supper
gathered one by one, each with his tobacco pouch.

Then Toyohara held his two fingers together
and began to sing a popular song,
several songs in a clear, bright voice.
At times he came to sing every second day,
at times every evening.
When it rained and he did not come,
the sound of rain took his place.
When the stars shone brighter late at night after rain,
he sang then went away, limping along the night road,
making the long journey home over the two passes.
The handsomest fellow around,
if he weren't crippled,
Toyohara would add another arc of colour to the rainbow.

The reason he came to our village every day
was because he was in love with Bong-Tae's elder sister.

The reason he sang on the heights of Soijeongji
was so that his singing would be heard in her house.
'Today too I walk on the evening road with no destination ...'
The reason why her heart pounded at this song,
pounded so rapidly,
was that she could not come out to see him
but could only hear the song with one deeply-pierced ear.
Once she got married, the song could no longer be heard.
They said that the sorrowful Toyohara went off somewhere,
kept his mouth shut tight, and waited for ebb tide.

—from *Maninbo*, Volume 1 (1986)

SEVEN

LIFE IS PROSE, DEATH IS POETRY

RJ: It is said that Pablo Neruda was the soul of Chile and Garcia Lorca the heart of Spain.

KO UN: Neruda was eventually assassinated by the Chilean military dictatorship, but it was a tragedy after he had enjoyed much glory and love. On the contrary, Lorca, in the time of Spain's popular front, was a still-incomplete poet who was executed in his youth.

Some 20 years ago, I was invited to a poetry festival held in Guadalajara, Mexico, and especially at a poetry recital in memory of Neruda, where I, the only Asian poet, read my poems and presented a poetic theory with five major South American poets.

I was interested in Neruda's communism, too, for some time. Because of his ideology, part of the American literary world persistently prevented him from receiving the Nobel Prize for years, while on the other hand he received support from Arthur Miller and others.

Fascinated by Lorca, I visited his birthplace in Granada with my wife to trace his life, after attending a poetry festival held in Murcia, Spain.

Dead poets come back to life in each era through their poems. Neruda, too, is still loved as much as he was

Time with Dead Poets

We are in one region of the universe, sometimes a
  wilderness,
sometimes a womb.
Now each of us
is not just an individual living poet.
Here
we are also unfamiliar backcountries
made up of something different
from living poets.

No sound passes beyond the boundaries of extinction.
Our bodies sometimes feel heavy,
sometimes lighter than our hearts.
The souls of dead poets
enter and make their abode in each of our bodies,
folding their weary wings
I am more than myself.
You are more than yourself.
We sing in the universe's dialect,
sing in the new mother-tongue of dead poets.
We begin alone,
then we are together all the time.

When huge waves rose suddenly
Only to settle back the next morning,
when the gulls emerged from hiding
after the terror,
no longer a-tremble,
and went soaring high, drawing the most refined
  circles,
a person died.
A poet, people whispered.

while he was alive. For some poets, life is prose, and death is poetry.

I love my destiny very much, the fact that I was born as a Korean and write poems in Korean. It is because I was a Korean poet that I was able to enjoy brotherly friendship with poets such as Allen Ginsberg and Gary Snyder in the United States and Andrew Motion in England. Friendship with them is almost that of a clan.

RJ: And in a poem you write: 'One thing alone is beautiful: setting off. / The world's too vast / to live in a single place / or three or four.' ['Your Pilgrimage', *Himalaya Poems* (2000)].

KO UN: That poem is from the poetry collection, *Himalaya Poems*. I made a pilgrimage to the Himalayas for 40 days in 1997, at the age of 64, aiming to visit Kailas, the holy mountain, but as a result of that journey, my body and mind became so weak that I couldn't write for a while. Several years later I wrote these poems.

Coincidentally, there is an episode related to this phrase. Not Vital, a major Swiss painter and sculptor who painted several impressive portraits of Nietzsche, told me that some years ago he got an English copy of *Himalaya Poems* from Hans Ulrich Obrist, a world-renowned art curator from Switzerland. Not said that he loved the poems so much that he carried it about with him for years as his favourite book before losing it.

Not Vital sent me an email asking for permission to translate this and two other poems into Romansch, his native language in the Engadin region, Switzerland, and include them in his own poetry book.

Last year, around the time when cherry blossoms began to bloom, he visited me with his poetry collection in his native language that contains three poems of mine.

At times, a day is as long as a slowly writhing
  intestine;
at times, a day is as short as a newly-born baby
  gull's wings.
It's because the dead poet's remaining lifetime has
  settled
inside each of our lives born of the egg-laying
  myth.

In the void above high plateaux at 5,000 metres
a dry, gaunt Tibetan gull is flying.
A very, very long time ago,
a continent came rushing near, collided.
Then what had been a sparkling sea
went mad and turned into the Himalayas.
The gulls lost their ocean.
They cried aloud.
They have continued their lives
through a second generation, a twelfth, even a
  1,302nd ....
Each succeeded the next.
And the next.
Their cries at last became songs, became poems.

So each of us
is a living poet.
We are each not only a living poet,
we need to be three poets, seven poets, eleven, in
  this world and the world after.
We are the very sensuality
of the time in which we come and go.
When we hold memorial for someone,

We enjoyed reciting them, each in his own language, in the living room in the evening.

Not told me that he liked my poetic leap of saying 'in a single place / or three or four' instead of 'in one place / or two'. Naturally, when I wrote the poem I was never conscious of that part.

A couple of years before we met, Not made a 14-metre-high bronze tree with the words of the lines, 'The world's too vast / to live in a single place / or three or four.' He installed it in the courtyard of his 1,000–year old Tarasp Castle in Switzerland and sent me a photo of it.

An infant crawls on four legs and later stands on two feet struggling, and that action led the human race to the path of *homo erectus*. Humans staggered a few steps and then started to walk.

While humans walked on their feet, opening up the world with all their might, each human being was a verb rather than a noun, and took moving from one place to another as an absolute necessity of life. They continued to survive by moving.

This poem is a condensed expression of that. It also expresses the wandering element in humans, the nomadic element, the uncontrollable longing for somewhere distant.

When I was a child, my father always scolded me for drawing birds, clouds, and sailing boats on the sea, rather than houses or mountains.

The places I've been to may be just a handful of the countless unknown places in this colossal world. The fact that the places I've not been to outnumber the ones I've been to often becomes my salvation and everlastingly makes me go back to my teenage days.

Imagination and dreams of unknown corners of the world are one of the sources for my poetry.

that's also the time when someone will hold a
memorial for each of us.
Our meeting here
is our leaving many parting behind
in many other places, elsewhere.

Here we are!
In our backcountry there is a lake.
On the water's surface, before and after we close
our eyes,
floats a white water lily.
Unfortunate is the poet who has never written an
elegy for someone.
On that account we must sometimes write a new
elegy.
That is another name for a love song. A flower.
Ah! we so need sorrow.
The lake remembers the middle of its ancient sea.

—from *Poetry Left Behind* (2002)

YOUR PILGRIMAGE

A slower pace, a somewhat slower pace will do.
Of a sudden, should it start to rain,
let yourself get soaked.
An old friend, the rain.

One thing alone is beautiful: setting off.
The world's too vast
to live in a single place,
or three or four.

Walk on and on
until the sun sets,
with your old accomplice,
shadow, late as ever.
If the day clouds over,
go on anyway
regardless.

—from *Himalaya Poems* (2000)

Places I Want to Go

Thirty years ago
I had places I wanted to go.
I was everywhere on a map
Of a scale of 1,000,000: one.
Twenty years ago
I had places I really wanted to go.
The blue sky that kept returning to me through
  the bars of my cell window
was my road.

Thus far I have managed to plod here and there.

But I have set a few places aside.
After I have quit this world
The places I want to go
will keep on waiting for someone to come.

I had places I wanted to go.
When flowers fell,
When flowers fell in the evening,
I straightened up, closed my eyes.

—from *Poetry Left Behind* (2002)

EIGHT

PEACE IS OXYGEN AND WATER OF LIFE

RJ: I know that you read a peace poem at the headquarters of the UN in New York. You suffered a lot from the atrocious war that broke out when you were an adolescent, and the war changed the course of your life. It surely has made your yearning for peace so urgent, so immediate and unusual that you keep talking about and singing for peace.

Ko Un: Yes, I had an opportunity to be invited to the 'Peace Summit' that was held at the UN headquarters and read a peace poem in front of representatives from about 130 countries. It was when Kofi Annan was the secretary general. The poem I read is about how peace is not just the peace for any one country or any one region, but it is a global and universal value and the rhythm of life, waving along all the seasides of the world like the waves. I remember that, probably because of my ardent reading, all the participants were excited.

When I was invited to a poetry festival in Norway, they organised a special event in which I read a peace poem with Johan Galtung, who was the founder of Peace Studies, in the 'Peace Park'. Whenever I am invited to an international poetry festival, even though the festival theme is not 'peace', I always include a peace poem in my list of

It's

It's a heart throbbing,
tears dripping from the muzzle of a gun.

It's
subtracting rather than adding up,
dividing rather than multiplying.
It's
listening.

It's
a bowl of rice.

It's
underground roots
not having to worry about the leaves up above.

It's
someone's childish fluting.

It's every kind of life,
each individual life
not subject to other lives.

It's
the sight of harnessed oxen plowing fields in days
  gone by.
Alas!
Oxen's millennial yokes.

It's
a father dying ahead of his son.

It's
a mother tongue.

poetry readings. I was also commissioned to be a Goodwill Ambassador for Peace by UNESCO, Korea.

I experienced the extreme situation of the Korean War in the early 1950s in my late teens, and survived the Korean War that lasted for three years and killed as many as three million, something unparalleled in the whole of Korean history. I have lived as a 'war orphan'. Therefore, peace is not an abstract literary subject. Peace is the oxygen and water of life, without which we cannot live.

The Korean peninsula is still in a state of ceasefire, a quasi-state of war. In the situation in which the two regimes of the South and North are confronting each other, peace cannot but be naturally an important and a grave theme of our literature. That maybe the reason I have written not a few poems of peace. I even wrote poems of peace as a series, numbering them.

Almost all secondary-school boys are familiar with the common knowledge that world history is also war history. Even in literature, war is never extraneous, and the narratives since the New Stone Age are almost all the records of war.

In the Sumerian *Gilgamesh*, fighting is emphasised, and it is the same with the Indian *Mahabharata* or *Ramayana*, and also with the Greek *Iliad* and *Odyssey* that imitated the Indian *Ramayana*. Although Homer showed a certain amount of war-weariness and cast light upon the horrors of war, by and large, the main goal of his works was the representation of the hero through war. What Homer wrote was a 'hymn', not an 'elegy'.

Since then, the primitive narratives of many peoples and tribes are almost all about war, making the hero of war into a myth. So much so, that even literature has made war literature its main characteristic. In ancient East Asia, the character 'dao' (道, way, road) meaning 'truth' is the image

It's
one person's blood warming another person's
  blood.

It's
a mother for whom her baby's crying is all.

It's
an archipelago.

It's a person being a human for another human
  being,
a person being nature for Nature.

It's
myself being finally abolished.

Ah, Peace!

—from *Belated Songs* (2002)

of 'cutting off the enemy's head and hanging it up', and of 'na' (我, I) the image of 'armed with a knife'.

Nietzsche praised war openly, and in some sense it was honest. War, disease and natural disasters have been even more necessary in the environment of human existence, and wars have been made crucial in the development of human civilisation.

Especially since the twentieth century, whether in the world wars or regional wars, humans have come to realise acutely that the formidable performance of the newest arms used in war could destroy the human race, and have sought for the realisation of peace through overcoming the war in order to prevent more destruction. Because the production and sales of arms instigates the outbreak of wars, the companies and the countries that benefit from the production of arms should be condemned and banished from the world, but it looks as though it will be a long time before humans realise it.

I defined war in my book *Forest of Concepts* as 'There is no world without war. / There is no world history without war. / Only a defensive war is a holy war, while I made definitions on peace as "War at rest"', and 'Peace is not a product of war. / Peace is only the product of peace.'

Although Nietzsche is my favourite writer and thinker, I always reject his praise of war. And I consider that Napoleon's cruelty and atrocity is half of that of Hitler. When I went to France I used to give frank advice that their pride concerning Napoleon should be taken out from school textbooks.

Armistice Line

Today again the sun is setting.
The tight-lipped ridges
and valleys are
opening wide their heart-hollows,
and the sun is setting along the 155 miles of the
  Armistice Line.

How I long to shout
like a mute, like a ...
What words could remain
at the ice-crusted headwaters of the Imjin River?
What could remain
in those Baekma Highlands, in Daesung
  Mountain,
in the rusted helmets below Hyangno Peak?

Fifty years of Armistice Line have passed in a flash
at the constricted waist of our land.
They have passed on wings beating quicker than
  agonised love.
There were days of snowstorm.
At high noons of hatred,
not minding who went first
they should have laid down their stand-off guns,
should have buried them
in the thick snow-flurries,
should have buried them all
in the day-long songs of cuckoos.

All those years every word was a lie.
All those years the roaming souls of the fallen
alone have bespoken the truth.

Fifty years of division have passed.

Today again the sun is setting on 155 miles of
barbed wire.
For what do I sing now, coughing blood,
if some day I should visit here again?
Don't blame me for singing.
Today again the sun is setting in silence. Darkness
comes without our waiting.

—from *Poetry Left Behind* (2002)

Peace 3

In the word
'Peace'
I see
bloody corpses.

In the word
'Peace'
I see scenes
of blazing shells in deepest night.
Didn't they acclaim it as fireworks on Christmas
Eve?

In the word
'Peace'
I see invasions and exploitation.

In the word
'Peace'
I see oil.

In the word
'Peace'
I see American airbases in Central Asia.

We will have to look for another word,
long obsolete or
newly minted,
a word no one uses.

Perhaps, the 'Shanti' of a dead language, Sanskrit,
the 'Kita'
of Malaysia,
that quiet peace,
peace for us all.

Also, the 'Pyeong-Hwa' of Korean language,
the morning peace that sustains those ordinary
days
when fathers die ahead of their sons.

—from *Full of Shyness* (2006)

PART IV

Dreaming of Poetry

ONE

LIFE IS A DREAM

RJ: Do you ever dream of poems, like some composers dream of notes?

KO UN: During my twenties and thirties I sometimes wrote poems in my dreams but I didn't put them down when I woke up, letting them vanish.

There are about a dozen poems that I wrote in my dreams that have been included in my poetry collections. They are mostly poems I wrote in my dreams after I reached 50. I just copied them down as I remembered them. Most of them have four or five lines, short poems, probably because they were made in a dream or maybe because of the nature of dreams. I realised that the poems I write in my dreams are different in length from those I write in real life.

While I lived in the mountains as a monk in the 1950s and then on Jeju Island, after returning to the world, in the early 1960s, my dreams often foreshadowed something that was about to happen to me, someone who had sent me a letter that arrived the next day or something that happened on that day. Solitude is truly the element of wisdom and the foundation of foreshadowing.

One day in the early 1970s I saw my father, whom I hadn't seen for more than 20 years since I left home. Later

A Song in Four Lines

When I open my eyes, flowers are blooming.
When I shot my eyes, rain is falling.

When I am alive, birds sing.
When I am dead, snow falls.

—from *Where Has My Countryside Gone?* (2011)

I learned from someone that that was the day my father passed away. In the late 1990s, while I was making a pilgrimage to the Himalayas for 40 days, I spent one night in a former capital city with an ancient watchtower at the entrance to the Takla Makan Desert, in a remote region of China, and I saw in my dream my mother, who looked young, as if in her thirties, and she was setting off somewhere. Later, when I got back home, I learned that that was the day when my mother passed away. The 'Concurrence' that Karl Jung talks about is a bit true for me.

Having experienced that the border between dream and reality in poetry as well as in real life is mostly unclear, I do not divide dream from reality clearly.

If we emphasise, as is sometimes said in the East, that the real world itself is a dream for a spell, it goes beyond the metaphor of the world and of the phenomenon of the world, and becomes a perception of reality. The phenomena of the world cannot exist without changes, and that accords with the changes and transiency of our dreams.

My first poem was titled 'Tuberculosis'. I wasn't ill with tuberculosis but I wrote it as if I were suffering from tuberculosis. It was when I was 24 years old. Then in the early 1980s when I was released from prison, a friend of mine made me have a check-up and I was informed that a part of one lung was calcified. My poetic imagination had turned out to be a fact. So there is the possibility of fact in fiction.

Now I want to come back to talking about poetry. Poetry is really both a fiction and a dream in reality and in life. The past found in poems is often connected to the future. My poems are sometimes the future that has come from the past and sometimes the past of the future that has just come.

A Short Bio

Now and again, I dream.
After a pelican has flown far across the Indian
  Ocean,
I dream.
Like my father back home used to dream
in the darkness when the light vanishes after
  sunset,
I dream.
Awakened from dreams,
I'm alive like a power line buzzing in the wind.

So far, I've always rejected dreams.
Even in my dreams
I've struggled to reject dreams.

Rather
I've rejected
every kind of fantasy,
any conjecture dominating an age.
Things as they are,
that's all there is.

Then I saw
a gleaming, the ocean at night
luminescent.
I saw
the waves' white teeth
glinting faintly
as they were buried in darkness.

Things as they are,
that's all that there is.
Yet I saw

Even though poetry is an expression created from the movements of society and of humanity's inner self, it cannot exist without the high-levelled and super-material grammar. The flowers on the earth touch the stars in the sky. The air and the universe of the dark matter that the flowers touch are, too, indeed the signal system they share.

RJ: You say in one of your writings that 'for a poet a dream is real life and real life is a dream'. Do you believe like Mercutio in *Romeo and Juliet* that dreamers lie?

Ko Un: Poetry is not confined by any existing reality. Poetry does not even leave silence at standstill. Poetry is a dance of sensations, of spirit, or of soul.

In ancient Asia, 'dance comes of its own accord, singing comes of its own accord', which confirms that poetry comes into being, not by a requirement or a plan, as a non-artificial and natural manifestation.

The peony that appears in poems written in the Tang Dynasty is not limited to that in Sian, the capital city of the Tang Dynasty; it can be a peony in the universal space. Poetry has more than one meaning fixed in each poem, full of elements of conception that give birth to other poems.

Poetry moves. It is kinetic. It is not a moon in a picture, but a moon that jumps out of that picture.

the glow glimmer then vanish,
a phosphorescence, with the oneness
of a new-born child with its mother.

Now I approve of dreams.
Things as they are, that's not all there is.
I dream.
Yesterday
is not today;
today
is not tomorrow.
I dream of tomorrow.

This earth is the tomb of experience.

—from *Songs of Tomorrow* (1991)

TWO

POETRY AND TRUTH

RJ: Can poems lie or does poetry come nearer to truth in life?

Ko Un: Poetry cannot be made only with 'facts', it introduces the workings of fiction that is the opposite of fact. Poetic truth goes beyond the limits of the factual concept.

Lies and imagination are sometimes one, even though originally there is a great distance between them. When I write, 'Last night I was in Andromeda', who could condemn it as a lie?

RJ: If we define truth as the purity of words, then we can say that poetry is truth, because more than any other human inspiration, it is close to the truth of life.

Ko Un: It's been some time now since an American cultural commentator defined the present time as a 'Post-truth Age'.

In reality there was profound scepticism about what truth is all along, since antiquity, and there has always been a debate over the true nature of truth.

As Goethe named his autobiography *Poetry and Truth*, poetry has always made truth its equivalent. Poetry has often moved away from the question as to whether it is true

10

It's best
when people can count as far as 10.
Once they go on to 11, 12,
utter disaster.

Ah! A lone child by the morning sea.

—from *Sea Diamond Mountain* (1991)

or not, and has not insisted on distinguishing between what is poetic and what the poetic truth is.

In the Gospel According to Saint John when Jesus says, 'I've come to this world to bear witness to the truth,' Pontius Pilatus asks, 'What is truth?' Here the truth for Jesus is the truth of God. This truth is probably not the general meaning of the truths we know.

In my *Forest of Concepts* (2009), published a long time ago, I wrote about true things and the truth: 'I support the truthful more than the truth.'

However, I often doubt and wonder if it's possible in this world to be truthful. We are now living in an age when poets can decide to be untruthful. In time and space surrounded by lies, errors, fabrications, subjective hypocrisy and confusion, truthfulness or sincerity might be impotent, old and infirm.

Until now we have used the word 'truth' without feeling especially burdened or challenged. Particularly, whenever a country's violence, invasion or expansionism were reinforced with fabrication and distortion of facts, there have always been political and literary sufferings in order to look for truth. Even justice is likely, as much as truth, to be a possession of violence and of the powerful.

For poetry to become a synonym for truthfulness, we need to have this kind of inner challenge. Nonetheless, we should pursue the truth that does not have blind faith in truthfulness.

In a word, not the bad practice of truthfulness but the renovation of truthfulness. A meta-truthfulness of this kind will do away with the 'poetry and truth' that has been accepted as an established custom for such a long time.

When Nietzsche declared, 'We have arts in order not to be destroyed by truth,' he declared that he had already left the banality of 'poetry and truth'.

In Metaphors Again

Child!

In order to express you, I have nothing but
  metaphors.
In order to express you
I have nothing left but my rotting metaphors.
Child who still cannot speak!
Child who still cannot speak
although you are five or six.

Good for you!

Particularity is a fact,
universality a sham forcibly composed of facts.
At times
it's obstinacy.

Tofu, made of beans,
doesn't last three days.
Eat it quickly,
eat your fill.

Don't trust your fridge too much.

Child!
Child!
The so-called modern, universal metaphors
  encircling you
are oh so antiquated.

Child who cannot speak!
Hurry! Scout out those unknown metaphors
that forespeak the language you will use.

Child!

—from *Where Has My Countryside Gone?* (2011)

Leaving aside the past days when we talked about 'poetry and truth', if we could see how the truth is being killed, since the fourth industrial civilisation, in a world flooded with fake news forged in real time, that dead truthfulness, the way truthfulness has been turned into ashes would be a fascinating subject that poetry should regenerate. Somewhere in the contemporary civilisation the search for truthfulness is drifting.

Poetry is a love song and a song of praise, but it is also elegy. The mourning here does not imply the end but 'the beginning', a rebirth. 'Resurrection', a poem I wrote in the 1960s, is about the splendid sight of the sea's horizon when dead squids, hung up to dry on lines by the sea, are reborn and start to swim back towards the sea.

THREE

A HEAVENLY ART

RJ: Would you say that this is the reason why poetry is a heavenly art?

Ko Un: Your classical question itself contains enough answer. If the question mark is removed from the question, it will provide the answer.

Only, truth is not eternal even though it is defined as such. There is no such truth or truthfulness. Change is the only truth.

Truth comes alive in a retrospection that reflects on and responds to all times.

RJ: Part of poetry writing is the process of rewriting history. How does this work for you in the context of Korean history? Is it a feeling of compassion or a sense of bitterness?

Ko Un: Especially in the 1970s and until the 1980s, I often dismissed any interest in the global or in the universal as an escape or a daydream, believing that such things were not part of a realistic concern for our country, people and democracy. I opposed a historian of ancient history, shouting at him to come back to modern history.

I was well aware that modern history is itself reality rather than history. Because of the attachments I had to

Looking Up at the Night Sky

Is the night sky a place where something new is
born?
Is that why the honourable stars are thickly strewn
there?

Persia,
Mesopotamia,
Ethiopia.
Are venerable Magi from those places on their
way, staff in hand?

I, too, simply cannot sleep following suit.

—from *Dokdo Island* (1995)

the ancient, ochre-coloured soil of the Korean peninsula, I had a very strong compassion for the Korean people, Korean *han*, kind of like frustration and resentment, and the incomplete and stagnant Korean history.

From the 1990s, I went through a mental reaction, escaping from being enclosed within myself, and that made me look up at the sky. The sky was the mother of the land.

'I' exist by action and reaction, according to the laws of gravity, an environmental system of the universe. Because of this fact I am first of all grateful to the earth.

Therefore, I do not refer to the sublimation or catharsis obtained in the ultimate state of poetry or of life as an angelic ascension.

I accept the praise revering Li Po, Hafis or Mozart as producing heavenly sounds, but my poetry takes 'heaven' or any mystery transcending the earth as meaning fundamentally the 'dream of the land'.

It was when I was four years old that I first discovered the stars in the sky. My mother used to leave home in the early morning and walk seven to eight miles to the seaside to gather edible seaweed, and would return home very late in the evening.

One day, while I was waiting for my mother, carried on my auntie's back, I looked up at the night sky, and starlight from some of the '5000 stars that human eyes can see' entered my eyes. That was the moment when I first discovered the world.

But at that moment those stars looked to me like some fruits we could pick and eat. So I cried, asking my auntie, 'Pick those fruits. Pick them.' I mistook the stars for something I could eat.

I never mean to degrade, by telling poor stories of what happened in my childhood, today's 'heavenly art' into something below metaphysics.

That Longing

See that tide rising in deepest night.
What is dying,
what is being born!
See the mud-flats late in the morning
where the ebb tide has licked the flats clean.
See the tide
flowing in,
ebbing out,
still unable to stop endlessly going crazy
for the moon!
the moon!
after how many millions of years.

See, then,
how industrious are the crabs and baby crabs on
the mud-flats.

—from *Where Has My Countryside Gone?* (2011)

Rather, my past episodes go beyond the borders of my present nostalgia. So to speak, for me the sky or 'heaven' is also my previous life in my imagination: the oneness of heaven, earth and man in a parallel relationship, not a vertical one.

Heaven, earth and man are the circular trinity of the world since ancient times in Korea.

RJ: Do you believe in an art of poetics in the Aristotelian sense of the term? I am actually more inclined to say that you get your inspiration from life and nature.

KO UN: I did not learn the basic rhythms of my poems from the multiple poetics and poetical theories that have existed since Aristotle.

After I returned to the secular world in the early 1960s, when the ravages of the Korean War had settled down a little, I went down to Jeju Island in the south.

When I was living on Jeju Island, I often spent a lot of time, sometimes all day long, just looking at the sea, sitting under a cliff by the sea. I looked at the waves that never stop washing ashore, crashing into the cliffs with all their might and bursting into fragments, that tragic destruction repeating infinitely.

Much later I realised that those tragic rhythms of the waves had become the rhythms embodied in my poems. My poetics is that of nature.

Earthly things always seek themselves in a different dimension, liberating themselves from the earthly limits and pursuing the universal. Responding to the sky or to the universe winds up my body and spirit with the electrical currents of the atmosphere.

The *gangsin* of Siberia, the spiritism of Siberian shamanism, might be a phenomenon of oneness of heaven and earth that continues in me, crossing the Tian Shan Mountain and the Altai Mountains in Central Asia.

I sometimes realise that in science there are in fact shamanistic spells.

FOUR

LISTENING TO POEMS

RJ: How much of your poetry do you 'receive' by observing, listening and inhaling, especially being the spiritually inclined person that you are?

Ko Un: One simple answer is not enough for this question, because there is an answer for each of the multiple states of poetry. Some poets can accommodate this question, but the path my poetry has taken is neither singular nor uniform.

There is a poetry collection, *Flowers of a Moment* published in the 1990s. The poems in that collection are often only two lines or a few lines, and this kind of short poem doesn't need to be revised for poetic structure or the development of a narrative. The poems are completed with the insight that comes in an instant's flash, the smallest unit of time. It is thunder, the sound of lightning incinerating the atmosphere. It is, so to speak, not rain or blizzard pouring down all day long. It is an immediate act of purification.

And the poems I write in my dreams disappear when I wake, leaving only one short poem in my head, so I write that down when I wake up.

However, it is the opposite in the case of a long epic that fills 1,500 to 2,000 pages of Korean writing paper, each page containing 200 letters. It is essential to have

Has a Poem Come to You?

I opened my breast. The lungs emerged.
Then, at last, the scalding heart.
That hidden future of a thousand years ago
and that all-too-hidden past of a thousand years
later,
both now have come forward to shape that mass
we call, today, a face.

Keynote speeches, poor debates.

Is 2000 part of the twentieth century or the
twenty-first?
Early in the summer of 2000
in the restaurant of a hotel
beside the artificial lake in Gyeongju
I was studying the water between the cherry trees.
The water was bordered
by too much falsehood.

To combat American imperialism from now on
we should unite,
Pierre Bourdieu told me.
He was three years older than me,
but very boyish.
So accordingly, I too became a boy.

The water was pretending to be unaware
of the lives and deaths held within it.

Today's face
emerges from two masses
lumped together,
France's then,
Korea's now.

an engaging patience rather than inspiration or insight, for the large-scale plot and development. Therefore, you can rewrite and edit ruthlessly, sometimes bringing back in again what you had thrown away.

Yet, it advances with only a vague idea, without any detailed project like the shots for a film scenario. It is automatic working of the narration.

Probably for modern poets, the life of the narrative is embedded in them as a gene, the life stamped in hard times of migration that continued generation after generation while the human race expanded across the surface of the earth.

Settlement began just yesterday, but prior to it the migration of the nomads filled the ancient times.

I believe that the veins of the rhythms of the long, long stories and songs that crossed the northern plains and southern oceans is immersed in my body and soul, too. Maybe that narrative instinct does not limit me to be a mere lyric poet but makes me write about the history of the vast plains outside my own cosy room.

Where I am, between my study and the world, makes the form and content of my poems different.

The artistic impulse that is often called *heung*, a kind of excitement, or *sinmyeong*, a kind of exhilaration, in East Asia is always burning inside me and keeps appearing and disappearing.

Heung in the hieroglyphics of East Asia signifies that when the god of the earth is offered a drink, the drunken god dances 'the dance of the earth', prancing up and down. From this it is said that poetry is the product of joviality.

RJ: How do you listen to poems?

KO UN: Some 300 years ago, a poetic genius, Kim Si-Seup, wandered among the Buddhist temples in the mountains as

Ah, the absoluteness of chance!
Just then
outside the window
one great-tit went flying off.
(A great-tit, I think, and not a sparrow.)
My attention,
leaving behind the heat of imperialism,
was fully caught up in that bird,
by the movement of that bird.

Bourdieu asked,
has a poem come to you?
(A bird just lifted off; surely a poem has come to you.)

Only then emerging
from beneath the expanse of water outside the window
I gasped, letting out the breath I'd been holding so long.
I replied as would a blind man soaked through:
Yes, a poem has come.

Together we laughed aloud.
When we laughed
the one had so many wrinkles on his face and neck
that the other's eyes disappeared completely.

Shortly after, Bourdieu crossed over to Japan,
gave a special lecture sponsored by the Fujiwara Publishers, went back to Paris.
Soon, he passed away.
I leafed through the 14 volumes
of the Bourdieu Library in the Fujiwara edition.

a protest against the cruel ruling dynasty. He wrote a lot of poems, but few have survived. As soon as he wrote a poem he got rid of it, letting it float away on the flowing streams in the valleys.

Roland Barthes said something like language speaks, not the author, in modern literature, and that the author's voice loses its origin when he starts to write. Maybe it's related to that, for in my case I hardly remember the poems I wrote.

I don't have any stubborn attachment to my poems. I assure you that I forget a poem as soon as I write it. Because as soon as I write a poem I send it away. Whether it goes to a reader or is carried away and reaches somewhere in the world, that is the place of the life and death for my poem.

When a poem comes to me I welcome it with my whole body, trembling with joy. In that moment I become a priest welcoming a 'messiah' in an unreligious, artistic meaning.

I approach poetry as poetry approaches me. Before a poem comes, my observation and empathy of the world and of the object as well as my sympathy and experience of the object are what I offer to the objects and also the objects give to me.

Ordinary poems, not the grand epics, generally come to me of their own accord, but I don't like the word 'revelation' that implies a heteronomy.

I think that my action of waiting for the time when a poem comes within the poetic magnetic field is also my autonomous action in approaching poetry.

RJ: Would you say that your understanding of verbal texture and timbre, of images and silence, comes from years of listening to poems?

KO UN: My physical hearing is very weak. Shortly after the Korean War, in my early 20s, I hated the sounds of the

Then
I read Derrida's and Said's memorial addresses.

Quietly, another poem came.

—from *Full of Shyness* (2006)

world extremely. Probably because I witnessed so many cruel acts of killing, I hated the sounds people made.

I even detested the sound of birds' singing. So I poured potassium cyanide into both my ears, in order not to hear any sounds, and I lost the hearing in only one ear. It melted the eardrum on one side, but as I turned my face because of the burning pain I failed to pour it in the other ear and instead it burnt my cheek.

In the 1970s, during the fierce anti-dictatorship movement, I was arrested by the authorities while I was involved in a civil disobedience movement. When I refused to make a statement, I was tortured and the remaining eardrum was ruptured.

Later, in early 1980s, when I was in prison, as the infection in that ear got worse they took me to a military hospital, where I had an operation to insert an artificial eardrum.

Now I hear with that artificial eardrum, and that is, at the moment, dependent on a hearing aid. In that sense I live with a part of my body depending on high technology.

Yet in my routine days I sometimes don't hear even very loud sounds and sometimes hear even a very small sound in an instant.

In Northeast Asia when someone is 'wise', or 'virtuous', we say that someone has 'good hearing' or 'keen eyesight'.

With that poor hearing, however, I cannot live without the poet's necessary hearing that should hear every kind of noise and roar, from the explosion of bombs to delicate sounds close to silence, or even the sound of an elementary particle found in the silence itself.

I conceive a certain potential of poetry from the sounds that I hear among the activities of life.

EAR

From the world
beyond
someone is coming.

Sound of rain at night.

Someone is going there. The two will be sure to
  meet.

—from *Full of Shyness* (2006)

Therefore, from the beginning it was just the opposite: the sounds of the world come into me and meet my poetry, rather than the world of my poetry turning to those sounds.

Hearing should not be the first priority before seeing, smelling, tasting, or feeling cold, hot, ice and fire, or pain. If hearing makes the other senses inferior, then hearing itself becomes a handicap.

Young Rimbaud asked poets to pursue the senses to the end: 'The poet makes himself a seer by an immense, long, deliberate derangement of all the senses.'

All of my senses including hearing make me advance toward the world in all directions. Only, since the present world is more inclined to talk than to listen, the hearing seems to need to be more acute.

The sacred act of hearing is the most precious attitude for a poet.

For a long time oratory has been dominant in the world, and thus people have been keen on hearing. Today people are keen more on closing their ears than on listening. In such times the ear itself is poetry above religion.

FIVE

POETRY-SONG

RJ: Can you write poetry anywhere or is there a certain space and quietude required to write poems?

KO UN: In the 1970s my life used to be like that of a guerrilla. So, when necessary I would write in the streets or on the table in a bar.

I was also in the forefront of the wall-poem movement that was something like the Chinese hand-written wall poster, and wrote impromptu poems on walls. And I would write for hours with a person who came to receive my writing sitting in front of me.

However, poems can be written as a roar of the soul in turbulent social movements or on the sea's raging billows, but also a poem can be written in the stillness of the tremendous pressure in the darkness of the deep sea where no light can reach. The poetic theory that poetry is the language of silence derives from that.

In the miscellaneous goods of the marketplace, poetry is actually missing. The frightening absence of sound following the end of the last movement of a symphony can be the beginning of poetry.

The Sound of a Waterfall

On the wall
of the Emperor's bed chamber
in the royal palace
was a magnificent fresco.
Within the fresco
was a roaring waterfall.

One night He refused to sleep with either queen
or concubine.

The following morning
His Majesty was irritated.
He summoned the artist.
Frowning, He spoke:
Two nights before,
and last night too,
I was unable to get a good night's sleep.
Why?
The roaring of the fresco's waterfall, all night
long,
was confoundingly noisy.
Blot out the waterfall, completely,
at once.

Immediately
the waterfall was blotted out.

The next morning His Majesty awoke from deep
sleep,
stretched widely
and said to the Lord Chamberlain:
Ah, last night I had a good sleep.

On the other hand, poems written at travellers' lodgements are often some lines or aphorisms scored by remorse.

Since the mid-1980s I have read books and written poems almost habitually in my study, a space familiar to me. More often I am a reader than a writer. My library is always a long, long womb transcending time.

I have transferred silence from a religious practice to a poetic action.

RJ: I have the impression that your poetry is very vocal. So, I am interested to know if you are conscious of your poetry as a spoken expression even when you are writing it?

KO UN: Poetry is originally song. Poetry belongs to music. In ancient East Asia, poetry was a composite art with a chorus as a collective action together with dance rhythms in harmony with the chorus.

Whether it was a ritual ceremony or the sound made by a river after a day's labour, the cheerful rhythms of the body and the meaning and notes condensed into the lyrics were all part of the performance.

Countless work songs since ancient times inevitably became poetry, as over the millennia mankind has lived a life of labour.

This poetry-song was divided into poetry and music as time went on, and dance had already become independent. But the nature of poetry includes the original musicality, the nature of dance and even the picturesque nature of painting.

In the colonial period of Korea's early twentieth century, the patriot An Jung-Geun said, 'If you don't read for even one day, thorns will come out on your tongue.' He didn't just emphasise the fact that we should read every day. At that time books were to be read aloud, even when alone. Reading a book aloud was the activity of the tongue inside the mouth. That's why he said that if we don't read, our

There was no sound of that wretched waterfall,
so my sleeping chamber was very quiet.
Cool!

—from *Where Has My Countryside Gone?* (2011)

tongue would get stiff and thorns would come out on it. Surely it cannot be explained as a physical phenomenon and encompasses the spiritual sphere.

Now, once poems were printed, reading poems aloud has markedly decreased everywhere except at poetry festivals. The reason why people gather at literary festivals and why poetry comes alive is because poets read their own poems aloud with various voices and gestures. The sound is what makes the festival.

Sijo, the poetical form of medieval Korea, originally belonged to vocal music and was performed at gatherings of the upper class for the appreciation of the arts. In the process of accepting the poetic forms of the modern West in the 1910s, the sound was removed from it and it changed into visual, printed sijo.

The lyrical poems as well as the oral tales telling the contents of narratives were, over a long period of time, a spiritual and corporal festival where its sounds united to the singers and the audience as one body.

This tradition has become almost powerless in modern times, having been turned into the inner act of silent reading. People are now accustomed to reading poems alone, without disturbance from anyone. Poetry does no longer live as a sound outside, but has become a silence bent towards the interior.

Modern poetry is thus an art centred on visuals. Mallarmé's poem 'Blank Page' may depict this heightened silence right before a poem is born.

You mentioned the vocal characteristics of my poems. It means that you see the potentiality of an auditory system within the visual system in my poems, which is also to point out my consciousness or unconsciousness about the vocal quality of language, producing from the mouth and going beyond the visual literary style.

In Lhasa, Tibet

I was at an altitude of some four thousand metres.
The Zangbo River sped by, fiercely.
A hat thrown in would vanish in a flash.
Turning round,
I slowed my breathing by half.

Following the octagonal path through Lhasa's Old
City,
I turned like a slow spinning wheel.
Such a crowd of beggars gathered, and so jubilant!

Among them was one old beggar,
all wrinkles
and just two yellowed teeth.
He laughed like a fool,
said only one thing—
not 'Gotta few pennies?'
or anything like that,
my goodness,
my goodness,
not that kind of dull begging,
my goodness,
my goodness,
but 'You're the highest!'

Just that one phrase.
In a word,
I was astounded, really astounded.
My poor wandering soul
was brought to a full stop,
awakened in amazement.

Here I'd like to make it clear that I never pursued any movement which focuses on vocal recitation as the modern Russian poets did.

My poems were expressed beyond the consciousness of sight or hearing, but probably they were already inwardly polyphonic as auditory language or for vocal language. This does not cut off the natural state of poetry, and at the same time, does not become indifferent to the pictorial and visual settlement of modern poetry, but remains the same answer.

I dream that my poetry will be strengthened by its inner visuality as it is more related to the sound and the voice.

There should be times when poetry opens and closes its eyes, listens and 'sees the sound'. In Mahayana Buddhism, there is Avalokitesvara Guan Yin, incarnation of 'seeing the sound of the world', or 'seeing the sound'. This Bodhisattva is originally an ancient Persian goddess, who crossed over to the north-west of Buddhist India, then, via China, came to Korea and Japan.

I want to write poetry that both hears and sees sound. I cannot understand the level of Avalokitesvara Guan Yin well enough, but I'd like to accept this Bodhisattva's 'seeing the sound' as fully as possible.

Yesterday, today, or tomorrow
never was there or will there be such a way of
begging.
No such begging would be plausible
anywhere else, anytime.
In the place I have come to,
in the places I will go back to,
in the world of thunder and lightning four
thousand metres
below,
who'd ever pay tribute to me
with empty hands,
saying 'You're the highest?'

Humbled by such extravagant respect,
how could I respond with a few pence?
So I fumbled to give him a banknote bearing a
portrait of Mao
and made my escape.
On reflection, like him,
I am doubtless the most wretched of beggars.
Days past,
and yesterday, too,
in order to lay my hands on a single line of poetry
and also on that space
between the lines,
I never stopped sucking for milk that would not
come,
like a hungry baby thrusting its lips against every
breast in sight.

It's been sixty years
since I first begged anxiously
for one word,
the truest word between words,
from some valley in this world,
from some slope in the world beyond,
or from some edge of the infinite
fathomless universe.

Spirit of one word!
You're the highest!
Dare I now hope to rise
to that peak of begging?
Only,
my happiness is that I'm no thief,
and my unhappiness that I'm forever a beggar,
that's all.

You are the highest.

—from *Empty Sky* (2008)

SIX

THE CHALLENGES OF TRANSLATION

RJ: W. H. Auden says, 'A real book is not one that we read, but one that reads us.' Maybe we can say the same thing about poetry in general, and your poems in particular?

Ko Un: Your enchanting question reminds me of a phrase, 'The more one loves the more one is transformed into the beloved', by the sixteenth-century Portuguese poet Luis de Camões.

In true poetry reading, in any meeting with poetry, the boundary between the poetry and the meaning of the poet is erased in a mutual transformation between the poetry and the reader.

Actually, I haven't said it openly because I feel rather awkward, but I have often heard at a number of poetry festivals people telling me, 'You are yourself a poem', or 'Whatever you say is poetry'.

I don't want to be carried away with these expressions and rather find them threatening.

RJ: Do you imagine a certain type of reader when you write your poems? Do you only write for Koreans or do you think in more universal terms?

Song of White

One life
dreams of another life.
Late spring white pear blossoms, their hearts
throbbing,
await the moon.

One life
resembles another life.
In the summer night, the field of buckwheat
flowers
awaits the moon.

One life
inhumes another life.
It's winter.
The snow that fell heavily yesterday
awaits the moon with all its heart.

I throw a stone.
Buried in the snow,
it begins another life.

Finally the moon rises.

—from *Belated Songs* (2002)

Ko Un: When I write poems I never have any type of readers in mind. I rather take it as the poem's destiny if my poem goes rotten or is expelled from where it arrives. I would rather leave the poem alone as soon as I have written it.

Or maybe it's the poem that leaves me. Probably that's why I hardly remember my own poems. If the poem survives where it flies to, that is also the poem's destiny.

Every day I have a lot of new poems that come to me and wait to be written.

The world in which I don't postulate the readers is the world of my wondering and flowing. My heart is just a village within the flowing circulation.

RJ: I have read your poems in English. Though I have never read them in Korean, I have the impression that sometimes much is also gained in translation. This is a difficult question, but does a poet need to inhabit an insular and self-absorbed literary universe to remain a poet?

Ko Un: For a long time, I have considered that poetry has, by nature, two paths. One is the blessing that my poems, written in my mother tongue and in my ancestors' language that I learned sucking my mother's breast, are loved in the land of my tribe and my fatherland.

The other is, furthermore, the honour that my poems are welcomed as travellers' songs in other places of the world where they go out unrestricted and are reborn in their sacred languages.

When poems are born, they sometimes stay where they are born and sometimes they leave for places far away. It's like that when a baby is born, it stays inside the room and then wants to go out into the yard and later to the neighbouring houses.

When poems are translated into other languages, it is inevitable that multiple linguistic sensitivities and

I Will Not Write a Seven-step Poem

Before a fearsome gangster-spirit boss who says:
'If you don't improvise a poem
while you walk seven steps,
I will cut off your head.'
I refuse to compose a poem
while walking seven paces
so say: 'Very well, here's my head ...
Now, off with it,
quickly, cut it off,'
and I offer my neck.
My head will fall
and go rolling, rolling away.

After which
a certain poem will restively roam the world
like some groundless rumour,
unjustifiable.

—from *Empty Sky* (2008)

layers of meaning in the original language are lost and that the meanings and the nuances change a little or even completely.

It is natural that a poem loses a lot of substance as it passes through multiple stages of translation. If a poem has power, even after it arrives in a foreign land, if it can make the readers instinctively imagine the invisible and delicate linguistic tissues as well as the whole body of the poem from the remaining bones, then, we may say that that poem is a good poem.

Only when a poem has the power to overcome the challenges of translation, will it be able to remain in multiple places on earth.

When I learn that my poems have reached a tribe in Africa or India and are read in their tribal languages, that my poems were translated into Kurdish and live in that land, I cannot but adjust my clothes quietly.

As far as I know, my poems have been translated into more than 30 foreign languages, East and West, now floating around in many foreign lands.

Surely it sounds fascinating to hear about an environment for writing poems in an island of the mind, isolated and doing nothing but writing. Some poets need that, but it has nothing to do with the environment in which I write poems. At one time I used to write not a few poems in noisy bars.

If I found myself shut up on an island while I write poems, probably I would immediately make a raft or a boat woven with reeds and leave the island. It just occurs to me that when Dharma of India escaped South China and left for North China, he used a reed boat.

For me, the time when a poem is born is the best possible environment to write one.

RJ: What is your stand on translating poetry? Have you ever tried to translate non-Korean poets into Korean?

Ko Un: In my younger days I translated *Poetry of the South* by Qu Yuan, who came from the south in ancient China, and also the poems of Tu Fu and Li Po. These are the only that I did.

I could do it thanks to the Chinese characters that I learned in my childhood, and also to the Buddhist scriptures in Chinese characters I read during my years as a monk. I undertook to translate those works while I was working with a close friend of mine on a 'World Poets' series project.

After that, translation has no longer been my job. I am rather destined to live as an author.

By translating the cultural legacy including poetry of all ages and countries, this world becomes more closely and completely one universal world, one global village.

Without translation it is completely impossible to live and survive. Culture is never pure blood, but a mixed blood.

Yet I expand the meaning of translation to something more than just the translation of languages. I believe that my poems are translations of the rhythms of the universe, of nature and human life into my own language.

Probably translation is the best element expressing the meaning of creation. All the art forms of mankind of all ages and countries that we are in contact with are imitations of nature or explications and translations of nature. They are natural selections.

I have learned the healthy start of poetry from Sakyamuni and Charles Darwin.

PART V

Death and Destiny

ONE

POETRY AS MEDITATION

RJ: If poetry is like spiritual meditation to you, then I suppose that you believe that writing poems should take place in absolute isolation?

Ko Un: Poetry writing is virtually impossible in the noise of the city or in the centre of the financial district or in battle. Even if you write about such a situation, there must be some isolation or creative process of filtration in order for poetic ideas to settle into a poem.

When Brecht depicted a landscape with smoke rising from the chimney of a lonely hut on the edge of the woods, he wrote about how much the landscape would look desolate without that smoke. I rather think that the desolate state before the smoke begins to rise is the force that brings the poem to the poet.

Solitude is a necessity in life as well as in art. Contemplation and solitary pursuit are also the physiology for poetry, ideology and discovery.

For me, poetry is not a singular kind of expression. I need a plural kind. I have never been faithful to the pre-modern sentiments of Korea or inclined to the narrative world of ancient Buddhism. I haven't focused the meaning

A Boy's Song

The reason why that sea without ancestors
breaks in waves like that, day after day,
is because it longs to become the sky.
It cannot be otherwise!

The reason why that sky
foolishly, day and night,
produces clouds
and then erases them
is because it longs to come down to the sea.
It cannot be otherwise!

The reason why I cannot live on my own like an
empty bottle,
why I cannot live only with kith and kin,
is because I long to become someone else, if just
once ...

Otherwise,
I'll have to live in ignorance of the countless
others
surrounding me in this world.

You people!
Marvel at the boy. Marvel at the boy's song.

—from *Poetry Left Behind* (2002)

of my poems only on the network of the complicated and confusing life of pre-modern and modern Korea either.

Nor do I want my poetic attitude, to which I turn consistently with one person's mind such as the contemplative self-illumination or the spiritual pursuit that encompassed the outlines of my religious experiences in my young days, to be the main characteristic of my writing.

Whenever I was captivated by a place or an era in which people live rather than by the people themselves, I was fascinated by the exploration of that specific space or the retarded experience of that specific age. Then, as I became interested in the fate of the people in that place and age, my mind reflected more on the faces and the shadows of the people, their life and death.

But I make it my aspiration that a poet should be free from the poem written yesterday. That reminds me of something that Hölderlin said: 'The poet is free like a swallow.'

However, I sometimes doubt whether such freedom is true freedom and whether it exists. Because I think that freedom itself might be another norm or regulation.

In the 1950s, Gongcho, a homeless Korean poet who was neither a layman nor a monk but lived in a temple, once said, 'Freedom restricts me.'

The more freedom is emphasised, the more likely it is to be fixed as an ideology of control. I always dream of poetic freedom where the border between freedom and lack of freedom disappears.

Furthermore, I ultimately erase even the difference between romanticism and realism. I long to eliminate the difference between advanced technology and primitive magic, too.

Today I am buried in spiritual isolation and taken up by the rhythm of silence following language, but tomorrow I could be completely different from today.

I could travel the earth, soar into the sky, or sing the various passive sentiments of life, discarding my own social time.

I tend to let myself be caught up in temptations from all things.

TWO

POETRY MAKES POETRY

RJ: Do you find it helpful, or even necessary, to meet other poets or writers or artists, as you have said in several poetry biennales?

Ko Un: Poetry is not a humming song one sings alone in a valley. I am a speck of dust that is always in touch with a cosmic phenomenon, big or small. So my dust-like song vibrates the strings of the universe everywhere it sings, even if the vibration is too infinitesimal to be a vibration.

Interaction with poets from different countries who write poetry in different languages gives some excitement and stimulus to my perception of the world and my pursuit of a different dimension of language.

When I meet a poet from another country, I meet not just his or her language and the works he or she wrote in the language, but a complex world engraved with the traces of that country's creation and evolution, its long history and culture and changes. Meeting with poets from various countries always impresses me with dazzling natural colours.

I feel happy when I discover the world anew through poets from other countries. I have a strong desire to take a deep look at not only the history of their homeland but also

A Certain Joy

What I am thinking now
is what someone else has already thought
somewhere in this world.
Don't cry.

What I am thinking now
is what someone else is thinking now
somewhere in this world.
Don't cry.

What I am thinking now
is what someone else is about to think
somewhere in this world.
Don't cry.

How joyful it is
that I am composed of so many 'I's
in this world, somewhere in this world.
How joyful it is
that I am composed of so many others.
Don't cry.

—from *The Road Not Yet Taken* (1993)

the nature and the society of their spirit and soul that have nurtured them.

Through meeting them, their country and society suddenly come near to me, and I feel my world expanding to the size of the world when I have not only poetic imagination but also the impulse of realistic inquiries through them.

If you look a little deeper, there is no country whose history is without pain and sorrow. This fact itself makes us consider that we inevitably need a solidarity through poetry.

I once served as chairman of the organising committee of an international poetry festival held in a city in Korea, and it was a fascinating experience to meet a diversity of poets from different countries. Eating, reading poetry and making short trips with the poets for a few days was a task of the heart, and I cannot forget the earnest friendship that bloomed there.

I had a joint poetry recital with Allen Ginsberg when he visited Korea. I then learned that the conservative social atmosphere of the United States had rejected Allen Ginsberg and made him a taboo. I also learned that his free and naked heart was the result of his pureness. The poetry reading with him later led me to meet with 'the Beat Generation' poets such as Gary Snyder and Michael McClure and the other poets of the younger generation.

When I met Allen Ginsburg in New York after a lecture at a university in the eastern coast of the United States, he advised me to not go back to Korea directly but to fly to California and meet Gary Snyder. But my schedule forced me to return to Korea directly.

However, later when I was invited to a poetry event held in California, I had a chance to strike up a friendship with Gary Snyder, whom I had never previously met. Gary Snyder, who lived in the mountains, had come all the way down to town to read my poems in English. I told him that

Allen Ginsberg, who had left this world by that time, had told me to make sure to meet him and that now finally I had met him. Then Gary Snyder told me that Allen had also told him to meet Ko Un from Korea. The two of us finally met through a dead poet. We had a good time together, saying that the hearts of one dead poet and two living poets had got together.

Coincidentally, Allen Ginsberg was a Tibetan Buddhist, Snyder belonged to the Rinsai (Imje) Order of Japanese Zen, and I once belonged to the Jogye Order of Korean Seon. In addition, we three poets were born in the same era (1930, 1931 and 1933). In a meeting like this, I discover destiny.

RJ: Which is more important for you: making poet friends at poetry festivals and biennales, or finding new translators for your poems?

Ko Un: So far, I have been invited to about 100 international festivals. When I was over 60, a civilian government finally took over in Korea, and I was issued with my first regular passport.

Then, I, by chance or inevitably, began to receive invitations from all over the world. For some years I received around 10 invitations in one year, and I usually accepted three to four of them.

When I first attended an international poetry festival, there were few of my poems that could be read in translation. Very few of my poetry collections had been translated into foreign languages because my books were banned from translation during the military regimes.

Then, from the mid-1990s, my works gradually began to be translated, and as far as I know, there are now about 80 books of translations in more than 30 languages.

Of course, because of the situation at literary festivals, it is difficult to make intimate friendships or aesthetic relationships there. However, I believe that fundamentally relations precede existence, whether at the level of the biological or anthropological phenomenon. The dramatic evolution of a single cell at the beginning of the world multiplying its cells is, in itself, an act of relationship.

When friendship between poets is achieved, ultimately 'I' becomes second to 'we'. It is not that 'I' comes before 'we', 'I' is born one by one from within 'we'. As I always insist, my poems ultimately become mine only when they are among other poems.

Meetings in literary events are much more meaningful for the friendships than for business. The friendships established at literary festivals have the power to sublimate the state of life.

Goethe emulated Hölderlin as a rival, but we can observe the friendship between Li Po and Tu Fu, 10 years younger, in ancient China. Tu Fu's poetics of yearning, his missing of the faraway Li Po, is resplendent.

Poetry makes poetry and friendship synonymous, and it makes life sublime in any period.

THREE

POETRY IN THE AGE OF SOCIAL MEDIA

RJ: Does it matter very much to you what other poets think of your poems after reading them?

KO UN: When other poets read and evaluate my poems, I am always uncomfortable and want to be somewhere else.

However, I believe that the boy-like purity that depends on such evaluation is very precious.

I tend to rejoice like a child when they praise my poems. Even if they are critical about my poems, I am hardly influenced by it.

I'd like to learn the sympathising attitude that other poets show to my poems.

RJ: Do you follow your poetic instinct at all time?

KO UN: My consciousness is often filled with many elements of poetic impulse; it is often excessive and becomes a state of inundation.

On the other hand, my heart sometimes turns into a landscape of desolate outland, leaving my sight asleep and cutting off my hearing.

At times I want to stay indefinitely in such a void. It's the void which is symmetrical to the space filled with people.

Singing Island

In the sea off my birthplace,
there are islands scattered here and there.
In a most haphazard way.
among them was the very tiny
Singing Island.

When gales came blowing off the West Sea,
always, invariably,
the sound of singing
could be heard around that island.

They were songs of the souls of fishermen,
drowned in storms
through the centuries,
who would wake whenever a gale blew
and sing for days, night and day.

As I grew up within sight
of Singing Island
some great spirit entered me
and I became a singer, still roaming today.

I became a travelling singer, awkwardly singing
awkward songs
with moments, though, of solemnity.

—from *Whispering* (1998)

So the oxymoron, 'empty fullness' or 'full emptiness', occasionally becomes my idea.

RJ: Do you think that poetry can have, in this age of social media, a real and lasting value for the people in the streets?

KO UN: I cannot hide my despair at this question. Our contemporary era, that you call the 'age of social network', overflows, in a word, with the totalism of the 'total age'.

The media dominate society, and society is rapidly changed by media, sometimes turned into a different form. To put it in rather harsh terms, a time of transition is not historical, but unhistorical. To such an extent, our daily lives are exposed to full-speed change.

The characteristic of the media is that it has the power to put violence to the fore. This violence is not only a product of a certain media system, but also turns the rampaging arbitrariness all over society into a sandstorm of things like hatred or order.

Institutions and social psychology are together fully exerting the theory of the evil nature of humankind. The truth, by nature, is variable, but it has long been buried in this overuse of media.

The universal value of truthfulness seems to have lost almost half of its effect now. Faking and duplication exert strong political influence not only on language, but also on human existence and throughout society.

Now poetry sometimes seems to remain as a kind of anti-social disease or minority complaint. I am not a poet who lived in a poetic golden age or in the glorious ancient times when poetry was dominant.

I want to bear the paradox of finding my *raison d'être* as a poet in a society where poetry itself has disintegrated and is likely to be left indifferently in the remote areas of society.

I want to be a poet who breathes my own existence at the edge of poetry for the marginalisation and the death of poetry, and not one who lives for the glory of poetry.

However, I predict that, after this kind of decline, there will surely come a sudden rise of poetry within the trajectory of universal circulation.

It will be neither chance nor inevitability, but the work of nature for the poetic infant to be born from the ruins of a civilisation, after the Digital Maoism of powerful social media confuses us by mixing truth and falsehood.

By the action and reaction of the gravity of stars, ruins give birth to the rhythm of ruins, which finally condenses the rhythm of the universe. Since ancient times, the East has spoken of the oneness of the universe and nature, which is right.

No matter how often people say that poetry will disappear, I think poetry will continue to exist on the scale of chamber music instead of symphony, as the solo performance of a single, small family.

In fact, Rilke's poetic activity in the 1920s was to hold poetry readings in the evening at gatherings of only five or seven people.

It may not be possible anymore in the future to celebrate poetry as I experienced in the mid-2000s at the Dodge Poetry Festival in the US, where I read my poems and talked about poetry in front of an audience of 2,000 people.

The sea of poetry is not the Dead Sea. Poetry will look for poetry only after having been starved for a long time. Therefore, as far as poetry is concerned, I should replace hopelessness with hope.

In fact, modern life is controlled by the absolute power of the visual. Our lives are dispersed by an excessive amount of advertising, entertainment and sport in real time.

In addition, only the mega-sized survives; small shops and items are to be found nowhere. Nevertheless, there is a homeland for poetry at the bottom of human nature. That native land revives alongside the shifts of civilisation.

FOUR

A POET OF TOMORROW

RJ: Is the thinning of language, which results from social media (such as internet language), a problem for poetry in general?

Ko Un: It could be. However, poetry has its own inherent resistance to such variables. Social language, the so-called primary language, and poetic language, the so-called secondary language, have, from the beginning, had a function of integration at different levels and dimensions.

It is extremely unusual for the language of the market and the language of life to be transferred to the language of poetry.

It is only possible through the liberation of a poet's language.

RJ: Do you know readers who have stayed with your poetry from the start and have a particular affection for your early stuff?

Ko Un: As far as I know, there are not a few enthusiastic readers who tell me that they have dozens of my books, including my early poetry collections, and some readers have the limited edition of my *Complete Works* published in 38 volumes in the early 2000s.

The Poet

For a long time he was a poet.
Children
called him a poet and
women did too.
Surely he was a poet
more than anyone.
Even the pigs and the boars
grunted him poet.

He died returning from a distant land.
In his hut here was not one word of poetry.
Was he a poet who didn't write?
So a poet wrote a poem for him.
As soon as the poem was written,
the wind blew it away.

Then all the poems of the East and the West, old
  and new,
flew away, swish, swish,
every one followed suit.

—from *A Cenotaph* (1997)

However, it feels quite undeserved and a bit unnatural if there are readers who have long been reading exclusively my poems among the works of up to ten thousand modern Korean poets.

I know that there are quite a number of readers and literary critics who prefer my early work, for its abrupt, ungrammatical and unexpected sensitivity. My wife, too, often speaks of the fresh shock she had when she read my early poems.

One critic said in an interview with a daily newspaper that my poetic sensitivity 'stood out' from other poets' somewhat bland poems. Maybe this is why some readers are attached more to my earlier poems.

However, while living as a poet, the poet does not stay as a poet of yesterday but becomes a poet of tomorrow. I, too, have gone through constant and radical transformations.

As far as I know, leaving the beauty and sorrow of my earlier poems that showed the presence of my immature youth preciously preserved, readers constantly love and pay much attention to the poems I have written in my middle and later periods. According to literary critics, most of my representative works belong to these periods.

I know that nowadays many poets actively run SNS (social network services) for the readers, but I dislike this kind of approach to readers.

My attitude to poetry is that it might even be better to break away from the readers. I am deliberately ignorant of the internet and do not send text messages; I still love to write with a pen.

What I want is to live on the other side of the moon. Sometimes I want to be absent, solely my poems existing. Poems written in the air and thrown into the air ...

Some old poems and songs were written by an unknown author or are anonymous. That is what makes that poem endlessly fascinating and likewise an enchantment attributed to poetry, undoubtedly.

Ultimately, I want to be a poem without poems and a poet without poems, and I want to write poems without a poet. I want to belong to the poem that is before or after language.

FIVE

POETRY READERS TODAY

RJ: Do you feel a generation gap between your poetry and that of the young Korean poets of today?

KO UN: A generation gap is a very natural basic ecology of living things. Poetry as part of humanities cannot be an exception to this natural phenomenon.

The Sumerian poem *Gilgamesh* written thousands of years ago is still read with considerable modernity in today's languages. Ancient Chinese poems and songs still touch the hearts of people even after 2,000 years. And Shakespeare who lived in the sixteenth century is not only in the canon of classical literature before the modern times, but also in the canon of modern literature. This is possible because they all keep to modernity with their literary and artistic characteristics, enduring the test of harsh times.

The energy of poetry, which has kept on existing through the ancient times and the present age, as well as the future of pre-established harmony, is disintegrated in a timeless manner under today's civilisation. So I think there is hardly any reason for us to have a fixed idea about the generation difference in poetry.

I read various books from all kinds of places and times, including the latest books about the theories of physics.

A Tavern

In the Sumerian epic *Gilgamesh*, composed around
  2000 BC,
a hero set out in quest of the secret of
  immortality,
killing a lion with his bare hands,
striking down a fabulous heavenly ox,
then pushing on to the end of dry land.

At land's end
of all things there happened to be a tavern.

Siduri, the tavern's alewife, said:
Sir, have a cup of wine.
Secret? What secret?
Drink another cup of wine, then go back home.

In reality, the ocean was rising in the haze
at land's end.

Oh my!

—from *Empty Sky* (2008)

Nevertheless, it is inevitable that there is a difference between the poems written at the age of 70 and 80, and those I wrote in my 20s and 30s, just like the different quantity of the brain and heart activities between those ages.

It is inevitable that the nature of my recent works differs from the experimental pursuit and the particular hues of today's young poets.

Youth possesses many questions, while answers get ahead in old age. However, it would be the role of poetry to break down this equation.

Not only that but, if there is hardly any difference between my poems and those of young poets, I would instead seek discrimination, and create poems completely different from the poems that come after me.

Wouldn't it be a mere factory-production if there were no distinction between the poems?

RJ: Do you have any anxiety about contemporary Korean culture alienating your poetry?

KO UN: No, I don't. My characteristic as a poet is that, though it may be a flaw, I am not conscious of other poems.

Nowadays, I occasionally read some of the poems that are nearly forgotten because they are either very far from me or very old. But I keep piling up gifts of books by recent poets. Their poems sometimes sound like mere personal small talks derived from shallow sensitivity and knowledge. However, I shouldn't say that there aren't poets that I keep an eye on.

I am busy internalising my artistic tension only with the closed circuit of my mind, devoid of others. This non-obsessed obsession of my arts might one day loosen up, but this probably means that my literary productivity has declined.

A Few Words

They don't disappear after weeping.

Damn it.
Damn it.
They're not foregone
with my body throbbing, aching,
after being beaten.

Even after a meagre soup of radish tops
at the end of three days' hunger,
they're not forgotten
as I gaze out at the hill before me.

Looking back, they've not been buried even by a
   century of
oppression.

A few words!
Sunset at sea,
I just can't help it before I die,
this accursed gift, stupid fluff, a few words.

—from *Empty Sky* (2008)

Perhaps, only then will I be able to meet the world of other narrators and other people. At the moment, as a poet, I am blind to everything but my writing.

As a poet, I am primarily an alienated being. However, I have never felt alienated from Korea's literary world.

SIX

THE PEOPLE WITHIN ME

RJ: You are famous for writing about those who are usually considered insignificant, such as children, farmers and village women. Do you feel closer to them?

Ko Un: After the 1970s, I discovered the people within me, which was never the case before. I became aware of the contemporary that generates an imperative nationalism inside the ecology of self-loss or else self-deprivation, which differs from the self-reflection of Western nationalism.

Because of this, together with the finding of the identity of a national society, I drastically came to concentrate myself on the lives of nameless people.

A worker's self-immolation in 1970 made me realise the sufferings as well as the will power of ordinary people and my poetic aesthetics went through a transformation. By accompanying them, my poetry had its turning point.

This affinity of mine with ordinary people was made concrete in my writing in the 1980s and 1990s up to the first decade of the twenty-first century when I was writing *Maninbo*.

In *Maninbo*, I wrote especially about the poor, the deprived, the powerless, the sad and the sick. Critics pointed out and appreciated the fact that the poems depict

The Women from Seonje-ri

In pitch-black, around midnight, the dogs
of Saeteo and Jeungtteum begin to bark.
Riotously.
When one dog barks, followed by another,
even the dogs at Galmoe across the fields join in.
Between the dogs barking,
endings of words such as -kka, -yeo, -da, -yeo are sometimes heard.
They are not unlike the sounds that the night's wild geese
let drop to the cold ground while flying high above,
harmonious sounds alternating among those in the lead.
The women from Seonje-ri are on their way home
from the old market in Gunsan,
where they take greens for *kimchi* from their bean-fields,
carrying the greens on their heads,
and, when they need more money, hundreds of garlic bulbs.
They have had to sell off what remained unsold at bargain prices.
It is nearly four miles from the market to their village,
and they have three miles still to go in the middle of the night.
The empty baskets are light enough, naturally,
but how light their empty stomachs must be,
with nothing all day to appease their hunger.
Still, they do not suffer alone.

mostly the ordinary and common people, and that they are placed in the foreground.

As I became aware of our nation and people, I constantly approached them, empathised with them, raged alongside them and felt very close to them, which I wrote in many of my poems but this is not everything in my poetic world.

As I am also a dreaming poet, I wish, on the other hand, freely and unceasingly, to wander along as the maximum, but also as an elementary particle in the multi-dimensional universe.

RJ: *Maninbo*, also known as *Ten Thousand Lives*, is one of your most representative works, depicting every person you encountered throughout your life as a poet. Do you consider it your best work?

KO UN: In the spring of 1980, officers of the Korean army illegally seized power right after the assassination of military dictator Park Chung-Hee. I had been participating in the democratisation movement for the past 10 years and was accused for conspiracy to rebel and violations of martial law, beside politician Kim Dae-Jung (who became president in the late 1990s), pastor Moon Ik-Hwan, professors, and others.

We were each imprisoned in a special cell at the military prison. It was an extreme circumstance in which death sentence was expected for at least five of us, in the ambiance of terror that reigned at that time.

I had to put together something for the end of my life. I even prepared a final statement and thought of my final posture.

The special cell was extremely small with no window, causing virtually claustrophobia, and I felt as if I had been put in a coffin alive. In this minuscule and sombre cell there were only a blanket and a urine bottle.

They share this hard life
with all common people,
with all common women.
What a good life, when they get on so well with
one another!
The dogs seem to have gotten used to their voices,
the barking diminishes,
and darkness blinks its eyes as if to declare, 'I am
the night.'

—from *Maninbo*, Volume 1 (1986)

I was inhibited in an obscure mental state, completely deprived of the present, the future sealed. I had no books to read, so I filled each day with memories, recollections, fantasies and daydreams. And then forgotten faces came to me from the distant past one by one, replacing the present.

The faces of the folks way back at my home village in the 1940s, my mother's parents, my uncles, and the village people came into my mind one by one, filling my dark present.

That later germinated into a poetic idea and project. I dreamed that I would depict those faces if I ever got out alive, and that dream became my strength to overcome the extreme time and the complete alienation. Constructing such poems that did not even have any titles, at that time, saved me.

After being tortured and interrogated, I was sentenced to a 20-year imprisonment by a military court and transferred to a prison in Daegu. There I lived in a solitary cell situated on the second floor, which was completely vacated because of me. A surveillant sat at a small desk in front of my cell.

While in prison, I was thinking of studying the Sanskrit of ancient India, but instead borrowed a Korean dictionary and studied Korean words.

In truth, I was subject to special surveillance, which meant that I was not even allowed to have a dictionary. So I had to fast in protest before finally obtaining one, and only then could I start to study Korean words. At that time, I came to realise that there were a lot of words that I did not know.

Later I learned that the Korean military authorities had accepted my request, considering the incident of Bobby Sands, an armed struggle activist in Northern Ireland, who died in prison after a 69-day fast in protest against British

Six-Fingers

Thirty years old, Six-Fingers was still unmarried.
He had one finger extra,
maybe to do more work,
so his right hand was always generous.
He was born like that,
there was nothing to feel awkward about, or anything.
With that six-fingered hand
he was adept at weaving mesh bags
as well as plaiting the big bush-clover sack
to put on his back-rack.
He wove big, round straw mats
while sitting with legs stretched out
and singing a folksong refreshing as a relish for drinks.
Whatever happened in the world,
he just kept on working,
no matter if some mischief-maker stole up
to surprise him with a loud sound in his ear
He just said:
'There's no way you'll ever frighten me.
Come on, eat this,'
offering a cold sweet potato, boiled the previous
 day.
Jae-Bong's father said of him:
'In our village, Six-Fingers alone has the very soul
 of a Buddha.'
Sweetly as he meant that, would he take
 Six-Fingers
as son-in-law for either of his two daughters?
Yeah, sure ... 'generous,' 'Buddha,'
nothing but words; noise.

—from *Maninbo*, Volume 2 (1986)

Prime Minister Margaret Thatcher's merciless refusal of political negotiations.

Around that time, I had pus coming out of my only working ear. After two weeks of fasting, I was granted an operation to insert an artificial eardrum. Also, my eyes became weak, so I had my eyesight checked and started to wear glasses.

After living for some two years under tight surveillance, I was pardoned and released.

With the influence of overseas life-saving campaigns by Americans and especially the former German Prime Minister Willy Brandt and then Prime Minister Helmut Schmitt, as well as domestic support and help, we received amnesty, and on 15 August, our Liberation Day, in 1982, I could finally come back to the world alive.

In May the following year, at the age of 50, I married Lee Sang-Wha.

As soon as my mind and body were gradually restored and stabilised by the happiness of my marriage, I began writing poems right away. Some critics said that 'an explosion of poetry' began in me around this time.

I started to write poems for *Maninbo* which were veiled somewhere inside me, and began to publish them one by one. Even while writing the poems of *Maninbo*, I worked on many other things at the same time.

So it took me 25 years to finish the *Maninbo* series with its final and the thirtieth volume published in 2010. It was 30 years after I first conceived *Maninbo* in prison in 1980.

According to the index made by the publisher, *Maninbo* contains 4,001 poems and 5,600 character names.

At the big celebration of the completion of *Maninbo*, American poet Robert Hass sent a congratulatory message. He liked my *Maninbo* poems a lot and wrote articles on

Sunlight

I really don't know what to do.
Let me swallow my spit,
and my unhappiness, too.
An honoured visitor is coming
to my tiny cell with its north-facing window.
It's not the chief making his rounds,
but a gleam of sunshine for an instant late in the
afternoon,
a gleam no bigger than a square of folded
pasteboard.
I go crazy; it's first love.
I hold out the palm of my hand,
warm the toes of my shy, bared feet.
Then as I prostrate myself on the floor
and bask my gaunt, unreligious face
in that scrap of sunlight, all too fleeting it slips
away.
When the visitor has receded beyond the iron
bars,
the room becomes several times colder and darker.
This special cell in a military prison is a
photographer's darkroom.
Without sunlight I sometimes laughed like an
idiot.
One day it was a coffin.
One day it was altogether the sea.
Amazing! A few people survived here.

Being alive is itself being at sea without a single
sail in sight.

—from *Fatherland Stars* (1984)

them, including in the *Washington Post* and *New York Review of Books.*

Encouraged by the enthusiastic reaction of many readers and critics, both domestic and foreign, it became my representative work.

However, my poetry writing did not stop there. Since then the world of my poetry has kept expanding to a world of other dimensions that are both more comprehensive, more universal, further away and at the same time closer.

Satisfaction certainly accompanies insufficiency in its signification. For that reason I'm not sure if I can say *Maninbo* is my main work.

What is clear to me is that I still have a lot to write, and I hope that the poem I wrote today would be the best one.

Memoirs

I was twenty.
World-weary for no reason,
I loathed the springtime when apricots bloomed.
I starved.
I wanted to fall
Bang!
on the bitterly cold snowfields
of Irkutzk in Siberia, forty below zero.
I wanted to fall, shot dead, like a young
  Decembrist.

In that obtuse period,
all I hoped for was storms that would jolt me
  breathless.

A shaking wrist was slashed by a straw-cutter.
When a hoe was thrust into the earth's flesh,
the earth went wild with weeping.

I was sixty.
I dismissed every kind of triviality.
Above all, I disdained belated excuses.
As ever,
I was revolted by lovely clear days,
had to run out,
rapt with joy,
to the far side,
to the far side of the plains
whose flesh through dark clouds was being struck
by knife-blades of thunder and lightning.

Away with every kind of resignation.
Away with every kind of nirvana.

Even after sixty, I have been inescapably, helplessly
childish.
All I have are a few friends,
and one lung.
I had to head in the other direction
on account of the lung I had lost.
Still I bear in mind Che Guevara, that evening star,
my belated
discovery.

The latter half is an explosion of the first half.

—from *Poetry Left Behind* (2002)

SEVEN

ERROR IS A DREAM OF ART

RJ: I'd like to know what you think about this statement of Paul Celan: 'Poetry can no longer speak the language which many a willing ear still seems to expect from it. Its language has become more austere and factual; it distrusts the beautiful and it attempts to be true.' Of course, one can understand why Celan said it from his tragic biography. But is it impossible, as Celan says, to write a poem which recognises the suffering of the world? I don't think this has been the case for you though.

Ko Un: Celan's jump into the river Seine is the tragedy of one poet, and at the same time it tells that a poet's life inevitably ends in the destruction of the soul framed by a certain state of extremity directly related to this kind of tragedy or even death.

I understand it in such a way because I myself had the urge to commit suicide and attempted it several times for 20 years until I reached my 40s.

When I imagine how Celan's poetic erogenous zone was wounded by the Nazis and the violence of war, and how his suffering soul of language struggled in cruel and inhumane circumstances, I can sympathise with the situation where he could no longer sustain his purity.

A Biography

I was born as a butterfly with a life
which might or might not have existed.
Very small eyes opened
to the light.
In the darkness
very thin wings came emerged.
Knowing nothing like the sea,
like storms,
that one butterfly
always alighted on the leaves of an overthrown
 nation.
It flew from here
there.

It was as if somebody knew from the start
how absurd immortality is.
In the fields where sunset alone was great
day was a colonised land,
night was my fatherland.
In those nights my forbidden mother tongue
murmured, unnoticed by any, inside my sleeping
 body.

Liberation came.
My mother tongue was splendid.

War came.
Among the ruins,
between the corpses in the ruins,
my blood-stained mother tongue survived.
I sang in that mother tongue.

His preference for truth over beauty implies that he felt, in a reverse way, anxious that the beautiful expressions of language could turn into lies, the opposite of truth.

It would be impossible that all poets stand at the altar of the suffering of Paul Celan, but I think that his suffering is not an experience unique to him. There is Auschwitz in his background, and even now there are extreme situations being created by other forms of evil in humanity here and there.

RJ: Have you ever felt you had failed poetry in some way?

Ko Un: Yes, I have. However, this realisation will exempt me from failure in the next phase.

It is my long-standing belief that in life, no achievement is a completion and every failure is a completion. We can say paradoxically that the ultimate incompletion of art is its true completion.

The error-like completion of error is a dream of art.

RJ: How difficult is it for a poet like you to accommodate language and mode of thinking to an unpoetic world like ours?

Ko Un: When I was young, I was sometimes buried in a self-negative state wondering whether or not I was a socially disabled person. There were times when I brooded over the fact that the childlike poetic arrogance of the night was irrelevant to the active life of society during the day.

In particular, a sense of futility or nihilism, which lasted for a long time in my youth, blocked my activeness or independent activities. Even when I abruptly exerted courage, it was likely to be a product of something unexpected, not of my own.

First of all, I am naturally a poor speaker, and hence, in the 'unpoetic world', my secular efficacy was all the more

My song was a mourning,
my song was someone's resurrection.
And my song was a song
of extinction,
not immortality.

I stood before dictatorship and guns.
My incantation
was several times imprisoned.
Contradiction
gave birth to narratives of contradiction
and lyrics rejecting contradiction.

Still that baby butterfly of days long ago
is dreaming at one place on Earth
of the truths of other places.
Life goes wandering on, inwardly unfinished.

One dream remains:
may the fossilised butterfly underground in some
  distant future
be a fossilised song.

—from *Untitled Poems* (2013)

mediocre either in my conduct of language or in between my consciousness.

However, since I went through a long period of religious practice, Seon-like intuitions may have taken root somewhere in my unconscious.

While I was practising Seon, fleeting and spontaneous language which is a flash of the mind or a magma of the primitive spirit, often rose from *danjeon*, the centre of the body.

The incompleteness of my statements to worldly questions may be attributed to the innate 'automatic narration' of my poetic language.

Probably the main characteristic of my language is how the reality of the primary language and the harmony of the secondary reveals their symmetry or asymmetry.

Long before Wittgenstein said that no sound of waves is heard in the word 'wave' itself, I was linked to the world of poetry where I could hear the sound of evening waves in writing the word 'wave'. It was because the language of reality had to worship my 'unreal language'.

Some days I am captivated by the urge to make a cocoon in my language, estranged from the language of the world.

Apart from the fact that modern literature reflects on the obscurity of language, I often experience how language is an instrument of error in all areas. The imperfection or error of language literally follows the complexity of reality. It is chaos.

Paul Valéry says transparency is a mystery, but I say chaos is a mystery. This reaction of mine may be what I learned from Seon, the immediate mind that cast away language and letters.

RJ: Were you surprised to be among the nominees for the 2010 Nobel Prize in Literature?

KO UN: I heard that some foreign newspaper gave me a nickname of 'a long-standing candidate'. Foreign media have reported that I was shortlisted for over a decade.

It's something that happens in a harbour on the other side of the horizon, so I don't know what is happening and what they are talking about over there. So I am indifferent to it.

Actually, my wife remembers that it was 2002 when we first heard about it. She remembers it because in the autumn that year, a large literary event was organised to commemorate my seventieth birthday (in Korean age), as is the custom in Asia.

According to my wife, a Korean newspaper called me to inform me of the news, and I relayed it to her while she was in her office at the university. Hearing the news, I neither rejoiced like a child nor coughed a bit like an old man.

Every year, people from domestic and foreign media gathered outside my home, and after the announcement at 8 p.m. in Korean time, they all left regretfully with their equipment. The silence of the night after their departure was rather bleak, but I grew indifferent as time went by.

My wife once told me that the Nobel Prize, though regarded a bit more honourable, is only one of many literary prizes in the world, and that there are many more important things happening in the world. We don't talk about it at home.

EIGHT

WANDERING ON EARTH

RJ: How important is the Nobel Prize for an experienced poet like you who has been through so many tribulations in life?

Ko Un: As a matter of fact, I have never answered such a question.

I sometimes think of what a great life of poets in the past led without having things like literary prizes. I think of *La Divina Commedia*, which Dante wrote during an exile in his later life.

Poets are sometimes the heroes of their age, but more often the heretics and victims of the age.

Li Po, a Chinese poet in the old days, said that poets are exiles from the moon, wandering on earth. His saying rings very true to me, who respects him as a big brother of my own blood.

RJ: Finally, William Wordsworth once wrote, 'In this very world, in this world of all of us, in this world where we find happiness or never find it at all.' And I wonder whether you've found happiness in this world and whether you are afraid of death.

Ko Un: First, I am not afraid of death.

Reminiscence

The wind blew for such a long time.
The waves broke for such a long time.
Wolves had been howling on moonlit nights for
  such a long time.

For such a long time
the sky was blue,
so blue and blue that it cried like an ox, like a
  worm.

—from *Where Has My Countryside Gone?* (2011)

More than that, death will surely be my final goal. I think any life is a completion in itself, but if life is incomplete it can only be overcome by death.

I was born regardless of my will. Therefore, I do not want to die with fear or anxiety.

One of my short poems says, 'When I die / I'll leave dancing.' The South African poet Breyten Breytenbach liked that poem.

In my *Forest of Concepts*, on 'Death', I said, 'Please clap, some of you, when I am dying.'

I live an immensely happy life with my wife. I'm living such an esoteric life of love to the extent that I don't even want to express it in words. My wife and I live a life where love and learning are dedicated to art, or art and learning to love.

At the extremity of the labour movement at the end of the 1970s, I tried to cut off all the private elements from myself, pushing myself even to consider family as evil.

However, the life with my wife Lee Sang-Wha, which started late, has always been a life in which the nature of happiness coincides with my heart.

My wife does not like me to say this, but if I had not met her, I would have died 20 or 30 years ago on a street or in a bar after scribbling some poems and drinking loads.

Society has given absolute meaning to the public by advocating 'public first' and 'perfect public' in the name of the society's virtues and values. This sometimes leads to totalitarianism and nationalism, becoming a regime that oppresses individuals.

Buddhism, too, has publicly expanded from fundamental Buddhism, based on discipline, to authoritarian Hinayana Buddhism, and later developing into universal Mahayana Buddhism aimed at the general public.

I think that the public is a reflection of the private and the private is the premise of the public, showing both sides of two existing forms, and that the interior cannot exist without the exterior and the exterior cannot be given any meanings without the interior.

These days I often say that the public is the total of the private, and the more private the private becomes, the more it becomes an element of the public.

I regard my family—my wife, my daughter, and I—as a private Trinity. This Trinity is over and above an ideological coordinate that was already created in ancient India before the Christian era.